DUFFY
DAUGHERTY

The mission of Greenstone Books—a name chosen to evoke the state gem of Michigan—is to publish works in history and environmental studies accessible to a general readership.

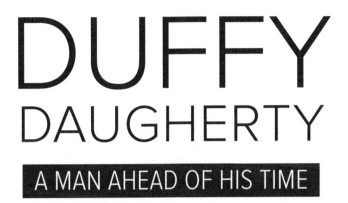

DUFFY
DAUGHERTY
A MAN AHEAD OF HIS TIME

David Claerbaut

Greenstone Books | *East Lansing, Michigan*

The paper used in this publication meets the minimum requirements
of ANSI/NISO Z39.48-1992 (R 1997) (Permanence of Paper).

Greenstone Books
is an imprint of Michigan State University Press
East Lansing, Michigan 48823-5245

Michigan State University Press
East Lansing, Michigan 48823-5245

Printed and bound in the United States of America.

27 26 25 24 23 22 21 20 19 18   1 2 3 4 5 6 7 8 9 10

Library of Congress Control Number: 2017963087
ISBN: 978-1-948314-00-8 (paperback)
ISBN: 978-1-948314-01-5 (ebook: PDF)

Book design by Charlie Sharp, Sharp Des!gns, East Lansing, MI
Cover design by Shaun Allshouse, www.shaunallshouse.com
Cover image of Duffy Daugherty, with 1966 All-Americans. *Left to right*: Running Back Clinton
Jones, Kicker Dick Kenney, Defensive End Bubba Smith, Pass Receiver Gene Washington,
and Rover Back George Webster. Courtesy of Michigan State Athletic Communications.

Michigan State University Press is a member of the Green Press Initiative and is
committed to developing and encouraging ecologically responsible publishing
practices. For more information about the Green Press Initiative and the use of
recycled paper in book publishing, please visit www.greenpressinitiative.org.

Visit Michigan State University Press at *www.msupress.org*

For Mike Emmerich,
a former editor and lover all things Spartan,

and Terry Vitiello,
whose friendship and encouragement mean so much to me.

CONTENTS

FOREWORD

Steve Juday

Duffy Daugherty was a great football coach, and his record proves that. The interesting thing is that he was a better human being than he was a coach. He was in a position to help young people, and he took advantage of that position. Recruiting football talent was his strength, but he did more than that. Young men with football talent and a need and desire to better themselves were his number one targets. Many of his teams were made up of poor kids from broken homes who knew their best chances for success was through Michigan State football. These kids were hungry, dedicated, and willing to put in the effort to succeed.

Duffy became the Michigan State University football coach at a time when African American players from the South were unable to pursue their dreams at southern universities. Duffy truly was a man ahead of his time. He offered these players an opportunity at a major university, MSU, one that had a reputation for accepting and nurturing young men from varied backgrounds, and it worked.

I have been asked many times about Duffy—his reputation, his persona, and his coaching skills. The truth is, everything you think he was, he was! As a coach he did everything right. He surrounded himself with a skilled staff, delegated authority, and held them accountable. He was tough but fair. Players and coaches knew what was expected of them and knew the consequences if they did not meet those expectations.

He was well connected. The press loved him and he was never without a quip. Other coaches were his best friends, and many players arrived at MSU upon the recommendation of one of Duffy's coaching buddies. Family and friends were his lifeblood, and he really enjoyed the recruiting process and the opportunity to see and get to know the families of his recruits.

Duffy may be best known and remembered for his wit, humor, and charm. He was at his best in front of a crowd. It didn't matter if it was a high school football banquet, a stag group at a country club, or the ladies' auxiliary at church. He could wow them all. His storytelling, jests, and jokes were always perfect. Following him to the mike was impossible.

Upon fifty years of reflection, I truly believe Duffy's wit, charm and humor overshadowed his excellent skills as a coach. Over these years I've been asked many times about Duffy. Most of the time people want me to tell them about the character, not the coach, but he was a great coach and should be remembered for that!

Most of all he was the greatest humanitarian I've ever known and should be remembered for helping countless people achieve their dreams.

ACKNOWLEDGMENTS

I want to thank Editor-in-Chief, Julie Loehr, at Michigan State University Press, along with Senior Acquisitions Editor Alex Schwartz, not only for their work, but also for their excitement over this project. My thanks to Annette Tanner, Digital Production Specialist, for her production guidance. Additional thanks to Matt Larson, Associate Athletic Director, and Paulette Martis of the MSU Athletic Communications department for their able assistance.

CHAPTER 1

Duffy

"Life has always been fun for me."

His name was Hugh Daugherty, but they called him Duffy. He was a short, squat man, often adorned in baggy pants, who looked like the lineman he had been. Often referred to as the "Irishman," or the "leprechaun," the Scotch-Irish Daugherty had an ample nose splattered over a large, genial face. Prematurely gray, he had the look of a happy, almost buffoonish fellow, one who had aged quickly yet gracefully. After serving as an assistant at Michigan State for seven years, he was the head coach of his beloved Spartans for nineteen seasons, although it seemed like many more. He and his coaching venue are inextricably linked. Michigan State football, Duffy Daugherty—they are nearly synonymous in the minds of millions of college football fans.

He was a great coach. Yet he is not remembered primarily for his coaching prowess. A racial pioneer in an era of civil unrest—unwilling to budge from his principles—Daugherty is far more renowned as a character. Incredibly charming and engaging, he was far more likely to laugh than smile, more inclined to quip than orate. He was an eternal optimist, the ultimate hail-fellow-well-met, lighthearted in victory and usually gracious in defeat. Yet he was a man not without pride, possessing a fiery competitive spirit, with an occasional flare of temper, and a capacity for candor and realism.

He was uproariously funny, a spellbinding storyteller, brimming with hilarious anecdotes illustrative of a life principle or referring to his Irish ancestry. One of his better self-deprecating stories involved an obviously fictitious happenstance in which he had a running feud going with an official. After jawing at the referee vigorously, the arbiter tossed his flag and began marking off a penalty. When Daugherty asked its basis, the official simply barked, "Five yards, Daugherty, for coaching from the sidelines."

"That just shows how stupid you are," the coach bellowed. "Coaching from the sidelines is a fifteen-yard penalty."

The official then walked over the angry coach, put his hand on the mentor's shoulder, and said, "For the kind of coaching you've been doing, it's only five yards."

Coaching, he never tired of pointing out, is not without pressure. "No wonder coaches get gray hairs, ulcers, and fired," he mused. "Players get four-year scholarships. Coaches generally get one-year contracts."

Among his favorite yarns was the story of one Pat Hogan. This tale provided both a "moral"—this one being about wasting opportunities—and a friendly slap at his Irish heritage. Hogan apparently devoted a day to touring a local brewery. While navigating the catwalk he slipped off the edge and fell headlong into a 30,000-gallon vat of Guinness Ale and was drowned. The manager of the brewery commissioned several of the employees to recover his body and he set off to visit Hogan's wife to inform her of the passing of her husband. When he arrived, he told Mrs. Hogan of the event that had made her a widow.

"Poor Pat," she wailed, "he couldn't swim a stroke. The poor man never had a chance."

"Oh no," the manager rejoined, "he had several chances when he came out to pee."

Because of Daugherty's engaging style and incredible sense of humor, he was far more popular on the speaking circuit than almost any other coach of his time. After games, writers all but fell over one another in pursuit of the coach to note his invariably quotable postgame witticisms. Coaching greats Hank Stram and Bud Wilkinson referred to him as "warm," "humorous," yet "honest."

He *was* a great coach. His nineteen years as head coach and 109-69-5 overall record outdistanced any other Michigan State football mentor in tenure and victories. He posted winning records in ten of his first thirteen seasons. Eight of those teams lost two or fewer games. His teams finished in the top ten nationally seven times. Between 1955 and 1966 his teams went 79-29-4, despite having to play the bulk of their games in the Big Ten against the likes of powerful Michigan and Ohio State. He developed thirty-three first-team All-Americans.

Daugherty finished either first or second in the rugged Big Ten six times, going 72-50-3 in league games over his near two-decade tenure. In an era in which but one member of the Big Ten was permitted to go to a postseason bowl—the Rose Bowl—and never two years in succession (which cost him a trip in 1966), his teams went to Pasadena twice and came within a game, or in some instances even a single play, of going several more times. Ten of his teams lost two or fewer games in conference play. He posted .500 or better records against seven of the nine schools in the conference, registering a solid 10-7-2 mark against hated in-state rival Michigan.

One of the joys of studying and analyzing sports is that it is so intellectually satisfying. Ernest Hemingway, James Michener, and David Halberstam, among others, have enthused and written about athletic endeavors. Yale professor William Lyon Phelps once stated, "Teaching is a great art, and the best college teaching is usually found in the department of athletics." Indeed, the highly intelligent Daugherty was a master teacher. His multiple offense, shifting defense, and constant strategic maneuvers were testimony both to his intellectual acumen and to his capacity to communicate his thoughts to young men.

Others of his time noticed his brilliance. "I'm not a writer," noted Paul "Bear" Bryant, "but I do think I know what it takes to be a great football coach; and I assure you that Duffy is a great one." Notre Dame, Texas, and USC, as well as the Baltimore Colts, Los Angeles Rams, and Green Bay Packers approached him about taking over as their head coach. He published two quality technical books on football coaching—*1st and Ten* and *Defense Spartan Style*—works reflecting clear explication, devoid of typical "coachspeak" pap. Moreover, his coaching achievements at Michigan State earned him a place in the College Football Hall of Fame.

He was in many senses a man of previous times, a bygone era, one of commitment to the most traditional of values. Intensely loyal, he placed preeminent importance on religion, family, honesty, and fairness. So different from today, he did not treat football as tantamount to neurosurgery. The legendary Wilkinson said, "Perhaps Duffy's greatest contribution to college football was his everlasting determination to keep the game a game and have it fun for the players. He may be one of the last collegiate coaches to keep the game in its proper place as part of the college scene."

He consciously balanced fun against competition. "I told every young man who played football at Michigan State that he need not put on a uniform if he didn't plan to have fun," he pointed out. But he never lost sight of remaining competitive, because for players every bit as much as coaches, "Defeat is no laughing matter," and it can be "a bitter pill to swallow when you know you didn't have as much of a chance to win as your opponent." He could say with conviction that in retirement, despite all the victories, "The thing I regret most about not coaching is the association with the great young men who play the game."

In an era similar to today in which coaches were exalted as mythic figures, often through deliberate image building, Daugherty was a man totally without pretense, never taking himself too seriously, yet at the same time ever conscious of his persona. "I always encouraged the players to call me Duffy or Duff," he noted in his autobiography, "and to call the assistant coaches by their first names." In a time of protest and student unrest, one in which long hair was more of a political symbol than a matter of personal style, Daugherty, unlike so many of his contemporaries, did not impose strict conservative codes of appearance.

"Personally, I never saw any correlation between short hair and victory," he related simply. "The only rule I had was that the players had to be clean and well-groomed." He believed respect was earned through matters of greater substance than rituals or conforming styles. Clearly, he was right, as the next rather extraordinary statement indicates. "I don't think it ever caused a diminishing of respect," he explained, "because not one time in nineteen seasons did I ever have to discipline a player for poor conduct on the field, and I never had a single player question my decisions on the field."

He had keen insight into the personalities of his players. "In football, or in anything else in life, every human being has a button," he explained. "It's up to the coach to find out what motivates a particular boy, you have to find the button. Now, you don't always find it but you try, and I think you sometimes try even harder with the young man who is more difficult to reach." Reaching his players, however, had limits, as Daugherty held the line successfully in matters of principle. For example, he would tolerate no profanity from his players.

One of his greatest players, Dan Currie, later NFL star with the champion Green Bay Packers, had a penchant for foul utterances. Great as he was, Daugherty put it all on the line after one of Currie's profane rages. "I warned him that if there came one more outburst, he could pack his gear and get off the squad." As Murphy's Law would have it, on the next play Currie missed a block with which he had had difficulty all day. The players waited tensely for their teammate's reaction. "He stiffened up, bit his lip, then broke out into a possum-like grin," Daugherty recalled. "As he walked back to the huddle he said—almost under his breath—'Excuse me, gentlemen.'"

This "Will Rogers in a coaching jacket" loved gags and gimmicks in life and on the gridiron but drew a sharp line when it came to matters of integrity. He refused to mislead recruits, manipulate players with hypocritical uses of religion (asserting that God has more important things on his mind than that Michigan State win a given game), or allow racism to go unconfronted. Despite the understandable temptation, he would not speak with college or NFL teams about head-coaching possibilities unless the position in question was vacant. He was loved. Texas coaching great Darrell Royal described Daugherty as one coach who kept "his sense of values—and still managed to win." John McKay regarded him simply as "a great human being."

He was also, however, a man far ahead of his time. That perhaps is why he remains so contemporary in the minds of those who recall his days at Michigan State. A shameless self-promoter, he was decades ahead of his era in knowing how to promote himself and his program. "I always recognized the value of getting the proper publicity," he recalled. "On the field you're a strategist, coach, psychologist, father, you name it," he stated. "Off it, you're a public relations man for the team, your school, and your community."

Because of his gift as an entertaining raconteur, Daugherty spent ample time on the road as a public speaker, using it to advance Michigan State football every bit as much as his own celebrity. "I never prepare notes when I'm going to make a speech," he said, perhaps stretching the truth a tad. "I always figure I'll think of something appropriate to say. When the day comes that I can't, I guess I won't get invited anyplace." He did get invited places, however, and State fans took notice. "It ticked me off good that when we lost a few games the know-it-alls came out of the woodpile and blamed me for being away from East Lansing so much," he said. "Where did they think we got those football players? The wider acceptance a coach has throughout the country, the easier it is to recruit."

He also saw the value of sports information within the university. "We always made members of the press feel welcome at Michigan State. I realized Fred's [Sports Information Director Fred Stabley] job was to project his coaches and the team, so I made myself available. I'm sure I was one of the first coaches to realize the importance of a good public relations program." Ever the ham and never able to resist an opportunity at humor, Daugherty would claim that while he always told a lot stories when the writers and broadcasters visited him on campus, he always watched closely to see which ones laughed. "Those who didn't laugh didn't get invited back," he quipped.

He was also a football visionary. More than three decades ago, he argued for a national playoff system to replace the polls in determining a national champion. He proposed the now popular statistical power ratings as a basis for determining rankings. Rather than having schedules drawn up ten years in advance, he favored imposing a three-year scheduling limit to accommodate changes in the competitive levels of teams. He presented an overtime system to avoid ties and suggested the use of instant replay to review difficult calls.

More important than any of the foregoing, however, Daugherty was a courageous trailblazer in tearing down the visible and invisible barriers for African American athletes, something about which he spoke openly. "I'm proud to say that Michigan State was a forerunner not only in accepting but in aggressively recruiting outstanding black scholar-athletes," he wrote in his autobiography. While the southern universities remained milky white, Daugherty headed south to recruit African Americans. He played them at any and every position—including quarterback, long the exclusive province of the white athlete. He did not care about quotas, restrictive measures, or any other forms of "politically correct racism" of any time.

Play them he did. In 1970, football power USC had seven black players, while MSU's 1966 team had twenty—including eleven starters. No other northern team of note came close to this.

Duffy had an "underground railroad" bringing southern blacks to MSU, but it was not just about football. He brought in fifty-nine black players from the South from 1959 to 1972, and 68% of them finished their degrees. This is a powerful statistic, especially in an era of segregation and "plantation coaching," one in which some coaches all but abandoned black athletes once the games were in the win column and the players' academic eligibility ran out. Duffy's loyalty was not lost on Jimmy Raye, among the first African Americans to start at quarterback for a major college football team. Raye calls attention to Daugherty's role in breaking the big-time football color barrier in his book *Raye of Light: Jimmy Raye, Duffy Daugherty, the Integration of College Football, and the 1965–66 Michigan State Spartans.* According to Raye, Duffy "had enough courage to be willing to coach and accept, to extend a branch to recruit black athletes in the South, to give them an opportunity to get an education and play Big Ten football. He was color blind."

Despite Duffy's unique efforts, John Matthew Smith, in "Breaking in the Plane (*Michigan Historical Review*, fall 1970), points out that he was blessed to have the support of then–Michigan State president John Hannah. In Hannah's first year, he desegregated all student dormitories. He went on to expunge all racial identification from student records, and on the athletic front, refused to schedule schools that would only play if black athletes were not participating in the competition.

According to Smith, the 1965 Michigan State national champions demolished the stereotype that teams could not win by playing more blacks than whites. The defense started six black players and five whites. Smith noted the words of Lawrence Casey, sports editor of the *Michigan Chronicle*, as he watched the 1966 team. "When the Spartans come out of the tunnel for pre-game or half-time warm-ups," they look "like Grambling or Florida A & M, don't they?" The Spartans opened 1966 with what *Sports Illustrated* called a "soul-brother backfield"—three African Americans and a Hawaiian. Furthermore, the two co-captains, running back Clinton Jones and roverback George Webster, were both black.

Other coaches had the political leverage to bring in black athletes at the time but chose not to incur the resistance. Rus Bradburd, author of *40 Minutes of Hell: The Extraordinary Life of Nolan Richardson*, referred to coaching titans like Bear Bryant—a Duffy contemporary—as "cowards" for postponing desegregation until the need for black athletes became a competitive necessity.

Moreover, the black athletes Duffy recruited were readily available to people like Bryant. Most were from the South. According to Smith, ten of the twenty-one black players on the 1964 team were from the South. Eighteen of the twenty-three returning lettermen from the 1965 national champion Spartans were black; eleven from the South. It is telling that southern coaches, including Bryant and Frank Howard at Clemson, actually sent talented black players from the South to Duffy rather than accept them on their teams. The late Charlie Thornhill wanted to play for Bryant, whose counsel in Thornhill's eyes was "like God speaking," but Bryant sent the Roanoke, Virginia, native to East Lansing.

Despite Duffy's benign relationships with African American players, the racial road was not always smooth for Daugherty. The Michigan State black athlete revolt in 1968 revealed his lack of sophisticated knowledge of the systematic nature of institutional racism. Nonetheless, while many of his contemporaries—like Michigan's Bump Elliott and Ohio State's Woody Hayes—lived with their own closet racism, or carefully conformed to the subtle but very real racial practices of the day—maintaining quiet but very real racial quotas, keeping the limelight focused on white stars to avoid the ire of white fans, playing inferior white athletes at certain more celebrated positions (i.e., quarterback), or simply keeping black athletes "in their place" by imposing tight behavioral controls—Daugherty's program was wide open.

In an era of overt racial antagonism, others were angry at Daugherty for bringing in African Americans in such large numbers. Duffy, however, was happy to take the heat when necessary, taking an unequivocal stand in the face of public as well as private resistance. Once when speaking at a golf outing some well-lubricated deep thinker interrupted his speech about the upcoming season by uttering, "Hey, Duff, how many niggers are you gonna start this season?"

"First," he said, filled with an unexpressed volcanic rage, "before I answer that question, if the clown who asked it is man enough to come up here, I will do my best to punch him in the nose." The room went silent and Daugherty then proceeded to explain in vivid terms his policy to play the best players "whether they happened to be all black or all white."

On another occasion, a generous contributor to the scholarship program hosted a party for the coach and his wife, Francie. The host turned to Daugherty and said, "Duffy, you've been using a lot of niggers lately. You know, the minute you start four of them in the same backfield, you've lost me."

"Then I've lost you now," the coach said tersely.

"Those are the last words I've ever spoken to him," he later explained. "I told Francie to get her coat, and we left."

Though he passed from the scene long ago (he died in 1987), Daugherty remains larger than life. His legend grows as the years roll by. No one old enough to remember his days on the sidelines will ever forget him, and no younger fan of Michigan State football has not heard of him. The giants of college football had their own unique and memorable profiles. Knute Rockne was a man of erudition and elite status; Bo Schembechler a grim, driven man; Woody Hayes, an often unhinged, volatile personality; and Bear Bryant, an obsessed, win-at-all-costs (sans desegregation) personality.

Hugh Daugherty was not erudite, not driven, not unhinged, and not obsessed. He is "a man who is at once interesting, full of humor and full of human concern," wrote Howard Cosell in Daugherty's autobiography in 1974. "Through all the years Duffy

Daugherty was more, far more, than a football coach. He has always been—above all—a family man and a man who cares about people. He has always, too, been an entertainer, a man who can tell stories for hours upon end and leave your ribs aching with laughter." Nonetheless, like Knute, Bo, Woody, and Bear, he is also one of the few football figures who is readily identifiable by a single, now-beloved name: Duffy.

CHAPTER 2

The Road to East Lansing

"I could have been a Rhodes Scholar, except for my grades."

t is often said, the child is the father of the man. Daugherty was not the son of a New York lawyer, a Texas oilman, or a Florida land developer with a veritable banquet table of ease lying before him. Duffy Daugherty came from mining country, more specifically the coal-mining country of Pennsylvania.

Hugh Daugherty was born on September 8, 1915, in Emeigh, Pennsylvania, but spent much of his childhood growing up in a neighboring town several miles south, called Barnesboro. Barnesboro, roughly 80 miles from Pittsburgh, 100 from the state capital in Harrisburg, and 150 from Washington, DC, is located in the western part of the state. The town was named after Thomas Barnes, who, along with business partner Alfred Tucker, opened the area to the coal-mining boom of the late nineteenth century.

Duffy Daugherty was the product of small-town America. Barnesboro has a population of about 2,500 and is nestled in a county (Cambria) that contains roughly fifteen hamlets with a total population of a little over 150,000. To put that in perspective, a full house at Michigan State's football stadium in Duffy's heyday would have held over half the population of his native county. Duffy undoubtedly learned early the credo of small-town America, that one's word is one's bond, that a day's pay merits a day's work, and that honesty and courage are among the greatest of virtues.

Despite his whimsical air and spirit of hilarity, the auburn-haired Daugherty learned early that life was serious business. His father, Joseph Aloysius Daugherty, worked in the mines and told his sons that he learned the art of tackling in a most unusual way. "We used to practice tackling by diving over a coal cart after a rat. If we didn't get hold of both hind legs, we weren't any good." Duffy's father raised chickens in the backyard, in part to feed the family. Duffy provided a glimpse into the compassionate side of his character when he noted, "I guess the toughest decision I had to make in those days was selecting which chicken we were going to eat on Sunday." Duffy actually had names for each of the fifty or sixty birds in the yard. "I really loved them," he stated, "and it choked me up every time Mom would decide to fix chicken. I could decide whether she should fix Janice or Lucy. The truth was, I would have preferred that we never ate chicken."

Daugherty reached great heights despite these humble beginnings. His role model may well have been his father, who left the brutal life in the mines to run the company store and then actually went into business for himself as a clothier. He also rose to the position of president of the local school board. Anyone reared in a small town can see the significance of this. So often people from rural environments experience a womb-to-tomb reality. They are born, raised, and educated in the same hamlet. From there they marry young, find work among the meager occupations available in the burg, and live out the rest of their lives as did their parents. Often the reason is not a matter of conscious choice but rather an absence of vision, an inability to see oneself in a context larger and more sophisticated than that of one's youth. Duffy saw change and upward mobility in his own home. He also saw the need to deal with severe economic adversity, as his father's business went bust. Although the logical and easiest way to handle the business setback was to declare bankruptcy, it was not Joe Daugherty's way. "It isn't the proper thing to do," said Duffy's father.

His experience with the hard edges of rural America, coupled with vision, likely served him well in his recruitment of African Americans at Michigan State. Many of these players were from small towns in the South, coming from families isolated by geography and the impenetrable walls of racism. Daugherty was able to communicate a vision to these families, a vision of their young athletic son heading north to play football in mighty Big Ten. Moreover, he was able to gain the confidence and trust of these players and their families, trust necessary to take the risk of leaving the parochialism of the rural South to venture into the unknown of a major northern university.

"From the time I was in grade school," Duffy recalled, "I knew I wanted sports to be a part of my life." Duffy got a sweet taste of the gridiron sport, during his grade school years playing for the "The Alley Eleven." At one point the team won twenty-seven straight games and played in front of large crowds throughout central Pennsylvania. Daugherty enjoyed recounting a perhaps apocryphal event involving a "sleeper play" called by his coach, Nutsy Fagan. It was so named because one of the Barnesboro players was simply to lie down, inbounds, at the side of the field so as not to be noticed by the opponents. The ten remaining members of the Barnesboro squad would then huddle, gleefully anticipating a certain touchdown when the skulker jumped up to catch a pass.

According Daugherty's biography, the six-point score never occurred. Instead, the local police chief, Ellis Davis, came sprinting onto the field, hollering in a deafening fashion, "Stop the game, stop the game. There's a man hurt over there."

"It was tragic at the time," noted Duffy, "but funny too."

In addition to his father, who played quarterback for the St. Benedict Athletic Club, Daugherty's two older brothers were topflight athletes. Daugherty himself claimed that his first Christmas gift had been a football. Often children with older athletic brothers grow up to become excellent players. They learn the harder side of competition by being beaten upon by their older siblings, but after surviving those experiences discover playing against youths their own age is far less challenging. According to Duffy, for nearly a decade, only Daughertys played center on the Barnesboro High School football team. Football drew particular interest in the Daugherty home, such that family meals were occasionally punctuated with Joe or one of his boys jumping up from the table to illustrate a disputed play on the living room floor. Daugherty's mother was not altogether passive on such occasions, but had to play one or the other side of the line.

Duffy was bright enough to skip the sixth grade and graduate from high school at the tender age of sixteen. There was no college legacy on which to draw, only a strong work ethic native to rural America. Moreover, Joe Daugherty's family needed to work its way out of the economic pit of business failure. Daugherty was unafraid of work, as witnessed by his labor as a special delivery boy while in high school. Duffy received 13 cents per letter delivered. He also worked in a bakery, and then at sixteen in the Phillips-Jones shirt factory. At eighteen Duffy labored for two years in the mines at

Arcadia. Mining work was incredibly difficult. Young Duffy arose at 4:30 and made the thirteen-mile trip to the mine. There he would gather the powder and supplies in time to be working at 6:00 A.M. Working in a three-man crew, Daugherty had to wear pads as he labored on his hands and knees amid about two hundred other laborers. Like another product of the cruel coal culture of Pennsylvania, Iron Mike Ditka, Daugherty realized there was little future for him working in the low vein of the mines. "Before long," he wrote, "I figured out there must be a better way to put bread on the table."

Despite a youth in the grip of the Depression era in coal-mining America, Daugherty later wrote, "Life always has been fun for me." He claimed to have enjoyed the simple, uncomplicated nature of life "in the rolling hills of Pennsylvania." Clearly Daugherty learned one of the most trite yet profound lessons one can learn about existence on Planet Earth: that happiness is a choice and that it is wise to make the best of any situation.

Energy, courage, hard work, and an upbeat attitude were soon to pay off in ways Duffy never could have imagined. Despite the grueling nature of his work, Daugherty's love for the gridiron was unabated, as he played semipro football on weekends for the Barnes Athletic Club around the state. "Even though we didn't get any money for it, we played with more zest and determination than some of today's athletes," he recalled. It was also violent, played with open-faced helmets. Daugherty loved to tell another embellished yarn about the toughness of sandlot football. It involved a young, 6'5" 250-pound Italian immigrant named Tony Mamone. The very rhyming nature of the name raises questions as to the authenticity of the story, but it is quite a tale. In any case, Mamone allegedly was hit, flew through the air, and landed on his face. The young man, out cold, with blood roaring from his countenance, was rushed to the miners' hospital in a nearby town. His jaw was adjudged to be broken and therefore wired shut.

During a postgame visit from Duffy and several other teammates, the physician informed Tony that he would have to be fed rectally. To which Mr. Mamone responded with clenched-teeth anger, "How can I have spaghetti and meatballs?"

The physician explained a liquid diet was in order, so Tony ordered hot chocolate immediately. Five minutes later the nurse returned, hooked Tony up to the rectal tube, and "served" the hot chocolate. The festivities had scarcely begun before the young man began screaming and thrashing about in the bed, only to dislodge the tube and send hot chocolate spurting about the room.

"Was it too hot, Mr. Mamone?" the nurse inquired earnestly.

"No, too sweet," said Tony through his pained and wired jaws.

One day a man named Jim Rorapaugh saw the Barnes team play. Rorapaugh went to Syracuse, and he recommended Daugherty to the Orangemen's coach, Jim Hansen. With his family now out of debt, the twenty-year-old Daugherty received an academic rather than an athletic scholarship to the university, indicating again Duffy's intellectual acumen—something he hid carefully under the veneer of self-deprecating wit—and willingness to work. Even this award, however, was something for which Daugherty took little credit. "I got an academic scholarship because I had good grades in high school," he noted. "I should have. After all, my father was president of the school board!"

By now, Duffy must have internalized several lessons of life: that life is hard, opportunities are few, and hard work can pay dividends. That he saw the glass of life as less than half full of opportunities is evidenced by his willingness to commit to Syracuse without ever seeing the campus, 350 miles away. Moreover, with but seven dollars in his pocket, Daugherty did not fly, take a train, or drive to the campus up in the Empire State. He hitchhiked.

That he took on faith that the Syracuse campus was what it was purported to be may be why he later made certain that he did not misrepresent East Lansing to prospective students. Some of Daugherty's contemporaries were a bit more "creative" in presenting the nature of the schools for which they recruited. Duffy wrote of Douglas Clyde "Peahead" Walker of Wake Forest, who had to go head-to-head with the likes of nearby Duke, North Carolina, and North Carolina State. Walker allegedly met recruits at the Raleigh-Durham Airport and then squired them around the Duke campus for their visit. Little did the recruits know they would see the Wake Forest campus for the first time when they arrived at the university to enroll in late summer.

Basketball legend Al McGuire, a man whose wit rivaled that of Daugherty, used a similar ploy at his first college coaching stop, Belmont Abbey in North Carolina. According to biographer Joe Moran, McGuire would buy postcards of the Charlotte Coliseum and send them to recruits, leading them to believe this is where they would be playing. He also used a brochure with pictures of the much more attractive Davidson University campus to promote wholly unaffiliated Belmont Abbey.

Later in life Daugherty enjoyed telling recruiting stories. One involved Michigan State's pursuit of Gene Donaldson, a stud of a guard from East Chicago, Indiana. Among Donaldson's university suitors were Notre Dame and Kentucky, then coached by Paul "Bear" Bryant. Since Donaldson hailed from a devoutly Catholic home, the odds seemed to favor Notre Dame—that is, until Bryant sent a priest to visit the Donaldson family for an entire week. The priest persuaded the family that young Gene belonged in Lexington and assured them that he would serve as the youth's counselor and guide.

Later it was learned that the "priest" was actually one of Bryant's recruiters in disguise. "I don't know what all of this did for Gene Donaldson's spiritual welfare," Duffy would say mirthfully, "but he became a whale of a football player and won All-America honors."

At Syracuse, Daugherty entered a "who you know" network that would serve him well the rest of his life. After going 1-7 in 1936—his only sub-.500 mark in his seven-year tenure, Hansen left after Duffy's freshman year, giving way to Oscar M. "Ossie" Solem, who came over from Iowa. Solem, who would coach the remainder of Duffy's days with the Orangemen (and went 30-27-1 over eight seasons), provided Daugherty his network in the form of two Syracuse assistants who have names familiar to college football fans throughout the nation: Clarence "Biggie" Munn (line coach) and Charles "Bud" Wilkinson (quarterback coach).

Playing guard was a difficult and often violent task in the 1930s, but it must have seemed an oasis of opportunity to Daugherty, who, after having labored on aching knees in the Pennsylvania mines, was now a young adult with a robust work ethic. Although Daugherty claimed to be "a very, very average player," he started as a sophomore on a 5-2-1 team. The team followed that with a 5-3 season in 1938, one in which Daugherty demonstrated his courage, if not his intelligence. In the fifth game of the season, a 33-6 defeat at the hands of Penn State in State College, the young lineman broke a vertebra in his neck yet donned a protective collar and played the following week in a 7-0 victory at home over Colgate, before putting the pads away for the remainder of the season.

Obviously, Duffy's character and leadership skills were already in evidence, as he was named the captain of the 1939 squad, one that went 3-3-2 over its eight games. Although one would not have been able to tell by being around Daugherty, life was not easy in 1940, the year of his graduation. Having majored in finance, he found some jobs available, but war was imminent, and the gutsy Duffy had his heart set on being an air force pilot. The portly lineman willed himself to lose twenty pounds, only to fail the eye test. Ever able to make the best of things, he coached the Syracuse freshman team in 1940 as a twenty-five-year-old and then went into the army. He coached a bit in Texas before being sent overseas. "I was no hero," he wrote about his war experiences, "but in twenty-seven months I learned some things about life and about myself."

Young Daugherty learned to go beyond making the best of difficult situations;

he learned the priceless value of a sense of humor. During his twenty-seven months in New Guinea, Duffy encountered a group of Australian soldiers who, after having endured so much hardship, would laugh at being scared stiff. "I was so embarrassed, and they were so strong," the man who received a Bronze Star of his own recalled. "So I started laughing though the bombings and strafings. Right then, I knew if I could laugh at all that, I could laugh the rest of my life, no matter what."

Life began filling out for Daugherty during these years. Before shipping out overseas, Duffy met a young woman named Frances Steccati one night in San Francisco. Daugherty had gone out on a blind date with another woman, but he became so enthralled by his conversation with young Ms. Steccati that his own date became angry and left. When Francie asked the young man how long he would be in the city of the Golden Gate, Duffy gave an interesting and revealing reply. "About a month," he said. "We'll be married by then." Hugh and Francie were married nineteen days after they met.

In 1945 Daugherty snared a coaching position in New York City at Trinity Prep. Meanwhile, back at Syracuse, a 1-6 season spelled the close of Ossie Solem's lengthy career as a head coach, one that began at Drake in 1921. The new coach was Clarence "Biggie" Munn, who, with the war now over, offered a young man named Hugh Daugherty $2,000 a year to join his staff. The network had kicked in for Duffy.

The Biggie and Duffy show ran only one year in New York. After registering a 4-5 mark, Munn headed for Michigan State, and Duffy Daugherty, now with a wife and an infant son, Danny, gladly accepted a $1,500 raise to accompany the ambitious Munn to East Lansing.

CHAPTER 3

Loser

"It is bad luck to be behind at the end of the game."

Founded in 1855 as the Agricultural College of the State of Michigan (and later State Agricultural College, Michigan Agricultural College, Michigan State College of Agriculture and Applied Science, and finally in 1964, Michigan State University), State was the nation's first land-grant college and the first to teach "scientific agriculture." Given its humble beginnings, the university has forever resided in the shadow of the University of Michigan, founded as the state university in 1817. Owing to its agricultural focus, State was often derisively referred to as a "cow college," "Moo U" (as in "cream Moo U!"—a sign proudly displayed by a Wolverine fan), or "Silo Tech." Athletically, the school did not enjoy the prestige of Big Ten affiliation (something Michigan registered initially in 1896) until 1953. In fact, save for Penn State, State was the final university to join the conference before its expansion in recent years.

To put it poetically, Biggie Munn had quite a run in East Lansing. His first Spartan team went 7-2 and he never looked back, at least not on a losing season. During Munn's seven-year tenure, State went a stunning 54-9-2, mainly as an independent. He posted a 35-2 mark over his final four campaigns. The 1953 team, in its first year in the Big Ten, finished as conference co-champions with a 5-1 log, 9-1 overall.

The 1953 season was also Munn's last as head coach, with Biggie choosing instead to devote his energies to serving as full-time athletic director. The choice to succeed Munn was his faithful Syracuse and Spartan assistant, Duffy Daugherty. As important as Munn was to Daugherty's career—"If it hadn't been for Biggie Munn, I might still be mining coal in Pennsylvania," wrote Duffy in 1974—perhaps a bigger benefactor was university president Dr. John Hannah.

Realizing that the football program paid the freight for almost every other campus sport, Daugherty knew he would need consistent political strength to sustain his post as head coach. Duffy, roughly as dumb as a fox, must have foreseen that working under his former coaching boss, Biggie Munn, a man not without a healthy ego, might bring some difficult moments. Duffy's love of the limelight was matched by that of Biggie himself, and now that he was off center stage, Munn might want occasionally to elbow his way to the front of the publicity line, throwing his weight around a bit. Duffy recalled some advice the great Earl "Red" Blaik at Army had given to one of his assistants, Andy Gustafson, when the latter was offered the head coaching post at Miami of Florida. The old redhead confined his advice to a single sentence: make certain you are responsible solely to the president of the university.

So Daugherty made a rather extraordinary arrangement upon his hiring: that he would be able to go directly to the president with any of his concerns. Hannah, whose tenure at what would eventually become MSU began in 1941, was wildly enthusiastic about sports and fully supportive of Daugherty. "Every coach gets criticism because no one wins them all, but I can truthfully say that Dr. Hannah's support more than made up for any harpoons sent my way," wrote Daugherty. On several occasions, Hannah talked Duffy out of taking other football coaching offers, regularly telling him he was important to the larger university, not just the football program. "Anyone who tells you he doesn't like to hear things like that is a liar or a fool," said Duffy.

Hannah's support of Daugherty was not rooted in altruism. He reasoned that a strong football team would bring much-needed recognition to State, moving it out of the shadow of the University of Michigan. "If it meant the betterment of Michigan State," Hannah once said, "our football team would play eleven gorillas from Barnum & Bailey any Saturday."

From the outset, Daugherty both embraced his job and defended the quality of the student-athletes in his charge. "The public has the idea that football is a game played by a lot of tramp athletes," he said. "Nothing could be further from the truth. I'm working with the best kids in the world. I'll match them for intelligence, loyalty—any of the qualities you like to see in young men—with any bunch in the world." He also saw his role as central to the educational enterprise, although with an interesting twist. "I have never made the statement that football builds character," he asserted. "Character is built in the home and in the church. But football will sharpen a boy's sense of values. He learns the value of hard work. He learns the value of being part of a team. He learns the value of playing to win. After all, this country was founded on competition."

Daugherty's distinction between the sources of a person's character is astute. He knew better than to be grandiose, taking responsibility for more than he could deliver. Indeed, he could *teach* the values of hard work, team consciousness, and competitiveness, but he couldn't guarantee that his students would embrace them. The gridiron was a blackboard, a laboratory, a classroom, but it was not a panacea for the male youth of the nation. He would be the role model, the whistle-wearing professor, but his students were responsible for internalizing his preachments, for adhering to his directives.

Hannah had been concerned for Daugherty at the outset of Duffy's tenure. State was entering just its second year in the Big Ten, having overcome opposition to its membership from its in-state rival, and had capped off its inaugural campaign with a Rose Bowl win over UCLA. In a three-way meeting with Munn and Daugherty, Hannah said, "It's a rugged conference. If you can win one more than half your games, you'll be doing a great job. But I'd rather you beat Michigan and Notre Dame more than they beat you."

In any case, with the president in his corner, Daugherty took over responsibility for Michigan State's football fortunes in 1954.

He would need Hannah's confidence, because Munn had left the talent cupboards rather barren. In fact, Michigan State, despite having lost only one of twenty-seven games over the past three seasons, was left out of preseason power picks because the Spartans were "starting over," having lost fifteen players (eight regulars) and three coaches from the 1953 Rose Bowl team. The team's principal holdovers included star running back Leroy Bolden, tackle Randy Schrecengost, and guard Hank Bullough.

Losing eight regulars in 1954 was not like losing eight regulars today. The 1953 season marked the end of free substitution and the return to essentially one-platoon football, in which a player played both offense and defense. More specifically, in 1953 the NCAA Rules Committee mandated that a player could not return to a game in the quarter in which he was taken out, except for the last four minutes of each half. The reason for this seemingly regressive step was the alarming trend of specialization in what had once been a genuine block-and-tackle game. "There is no doubt that the most efficient way to play football is through the medium of free substitution" noted *Sports Illustrated*'s football writer Herman Hickman in 1954. "However, by 1952 the offensive and defensive units had evolved into punting teams, kickoff returning and covering groups, and extra point units. In another few years, if the Rules Committee had not wisely stepped in, there is no telling just how far the specialization would have gone."

Cries of a "return to the Dark Ages" and "horse-and-buggy football" were heard around the nation. Schools like Notre Dame and Army that had stockpiled players were particularly unhappy because this cut into their advantage, rooted in depth of talent. As it turned out, in 1953 the power teams remained powerful and the weak, weak. Columbia's venerable Lou Little put the case of the latter well when he said, "There is no legislation that will help an inferior football team."

Duffy's first game was a grinder. Leading at Iowa City with less than eight minutes to go against the #4-ranked Hawkeyes, he watched Iowa star quarterback Jerry Reichow, facing a fourth down, sneak over the chalk line to give the home team a 14-10 win and Daugherty an 0-1 record.

There was no time to hang one's head, because mighty #3 Wisconsin was coming to East Lansing next. This one was even more painful. In a fierce defensive struggle, the Badgers got the game's only touchdown while State, amid a substitution mix-up, had only ten men on the field. The final score was an agonizing 6-0.

Indiana provided a potential respite for the battle-tested Spartans in Bloomington a week later. Duffy's charges responded giving him his first win as a head coach, 21-14.

Game four would also be played in Indiana, but not against the Hoosiers. It would pit the Green and White against mighty Notre Dame, one of the two teams President Hannah had cited as especially important to defeat. Duffy had his team ready, and in a slug-it-out battle in the mud and rain, the Spartans stood tall. But not quite tall enough. With State up 13-0 in the first quarter, the #6 Irish, behind Joe Heap and Don Schaefer, fought back to register a 20-19 victory.

Facing the middle game in a nine-game season, the Spartans were 1-3 but had yet to lose a game by more than 6 points. After the first four, they had been outscored only 54-50.

A tough, #9 Purdue came into East Lansing a week later and left having scored 27 points against State's 13. Two straight losses begat another as the Spartans fell 19-13 at Minnesota a week later.

Facing what looked like a freefall, Duffy got his team ready to play a mediocre Washington State team at home. The prrepared Spartans rolled to a thunderous 54-6 win. This ability to turn a battle-weary team around would mark Daugherty's coaching throughout his tenure at State. His teams were never to be taken for granted. Although he won far more than he lost, he did occasionally have some subpar teams, but almost without exception he would pull a rabbit or two out of his coaching hat with those groups and register surprising victories.

Part of the reason, perhaps, is that life was always fun for Duffy. At least, he did the best to make it fun for himself and, more important, for those around him. "Have some fun out there," he would yell to his players at practice. That happy attitude, that joyous outlook, likely infected his team sufficiently to rise above the dregs of defeatism and the temptation to "mail it in" once a season seemed certain to be a loser. Daugherty always sought to put a team on the gridiron that was ready to play, that could not wait another second to get it on with the next opponent. To that end, his policy was not to scrimmage his regulars after the season had begun. Whereas other grim-faced mentors would make their teams "hit" almost as a punishment for a poor game the week before, Daugherty believed his squads would be far hungrier if he bottled up that urge until his charges encountered players with different uniforms on game day.

He was also one very sharp football man. In an era of autocratic control, Daugherty was again ahead of his time, giving his seven or so assistants complete authority in their areas of specialization. He also allowed them to speak openly to the press, unheard of in the 1950s. "Duffy claims there are no geniuses in coaching," one of his assistants said in 1956. "I don't know, but sometimes he almost acts like one. There'll be a problem, for instance. All of us will know all the elements of the problem; have all the facts necessary for a solution. But we sit there baffled until Duffy comes along, looks at the facts and sees the way out that we couldn't see. That's why, whenever things look bad, we always say, 'Duffy will think of something.'"

He couldn't think of much in his first encounter with the Michigan at the Big House, however. Although he went 10-7-2 against the hated Wolverines over his career at State, his initial confrontation with his archrivals was less than auspicious, as the Wolverines, led by All-American Ron Kramer—who among other things stuffed two punts—pulverized the Spartans 33-7 on four second-half touchdowns.

The finale of Duffy's first season as head coach was against a 3-4-1 Marquette team in East Lansing. The Catholic school from Milwaukee was no match for the Big Ten–hardened Spartans, as State closed the 1954 books with a rousing 40-10 romp.

Duffy Daugherty's first team went 3-6-0, and an even worse 1-5 as defending co-champions of the Big Ten. It was a bitter start to his career as head coach, a year in which the Spartans lost four games by 6 points or less. In fact, the 3-6 squad actually outscored the opposition for the season, 177-149. Particularly galling was the 14-10 loss in the opener at Iowa, in addition to a midseason 20-19 upending at hated Notre Dame. Every team to which the Spartans lost finished the year with a winning record. The overall mark of those six opponents was 39-15-1. Nevertheless, Duffy had turned in the first losing season since he and Biggie Munn had come to East Lansing eight years before.

Tied for 8th in the Big Ten with that 1-5 mark, the Spartans were 7th in total offense and 8th on defense. They were –4 in turnover margin. With no individual statistical standouts other than John Matsock's leading the Big Ten in kickoff returns (21.8 average), no Spartan made either the first or second all-conference team.

Daugherty was now much in the shadow of the never-losing Biggie Munn. There were questions as to whether the thirty-nine-year-old was up to the job, had the right stuff to fill Munn's gigantic shoes. And Munn was a giant. He had taken over the State coaching job in 1947, and by 1953, the forty-five-year-old resigned to take over as athletic director, already having won a national championship in 1952, a Big Ten co-championship in his first and only season in the conference (1953), and a Rose Bowl date after the title season, with a stunning overall record of 54-9-2. For Munn, Duffy would always be his underling. After all, he had coached him in college, hired him as his assistant during his one season at Syracuse, and then taken Duffy along for his glorious seven-year ride at State. As far as Munn was concerned, he was more than Daugherty's mentor and superior. He was the reason Duffy was a coach at all.

Daugherty had a conflicted set of emotions with regard to Munn. Indeed, he acknowledged that there would be no Hugh "Duffy" Daugherty, head coach at Michigan State, without Munn. The problem, however, lay in Munn's insufferable ego and his desire to subordinate Daugherty such that Duffy, a man who thirsted for attention much as did Munn, couldn't really be his own man. It was for this reason, the desire to get out from under Munn, that Daugherty struck his deal with Hannah. It was also why Duffy did not look to his former boss for counsel when State fell upon hard times in 1954. Munn's office door was "always open whenever he wanted to talk football," but Duffy did not walk through it, and Munn did not like Duffy's independence.

CHAPTER 4

Pasadena Bound

"Some people who didn't wear face guards haven't got teeth."

—Daugherty's retort to Athletic Director Biggie Munn and others' criticisms of the modern helmets

To manage what had become a potentially career-threatening situation, the ever-cagey Daugherty wisely cried the blues as the 1955 season approached. Having lost nineteen lettermen from his inaugural team, Duffy made certain little was expected. "We haven't had a squad this green in years," he remarked. "No wonder the writers are playing us down this fall. It figures."

Nobody was very impressed when Michigan State opened the season by downing Indiana, a team on its way to a 3-6 season, before a crowd estimated at 23,000. The score was 20-13.

The next game, however, garnered greater attention. It pitted State against the mighty Wolverines, again in Ann Arbor's Big House. Michigan State was a thirteen-point underdog. Daugherty, as he team practiced during the week, was concerned about Wolverine great Ron Kramer. A high jumper in track, a sixteen-point-a-game star in basketball, the 6'3" 222-pound Kramer punted, kicked off, place-kicked, ran the end-around, and caught passes for Michigan. As concerned as he was about Kramer and the Wolverine air game, Duffy didn't lose sight of the other side of the ball. "What you've got to remember is Michigan's defense," he told one writer that week. "They keep the pressure right on you. And when they get an opening they really hurt you."

The intrastate game had developed into a substantial rivalry over the years. Before the game the campus was adorned here and there with hand-lettered signs saying, "CREAM MOO U." The pep rally and bonfire the night before the game evolved into a loud panty raid. The Wolverines, coached by Bennie Oosterbaan, came into the game as the Big Ten favorite, having mauled Missouri 42-7 in the opener. Daugherty, however, had worked his positive-attitude psychological magic. "Our boys wanted to win this one more than any other," he said after the game. "We came down here expecting to win." To drive up the fervor, President Hannah had come out to practice to address the Spartans.

The crowd, numbering 97,239, piled into the stadium built in 1927, the year Oosterbaan had captained the Wolverines. They watched with dismay as Walt Kowalczyk fielded the opening kick and ran it out to the thirty-nine. Duffy, having put together a complex offense, one that used the T and the single wing behind an unbalanced line, watched his team pick up a quick first down on the Michigan forty-nine. Ace quarterback Earl Morrall then dropped back and to his left to throw. Unfortunately, he was picked off by Michigan's Tony Branoff in the flat, and he raced down to the Spartan twenty with the pigskin. Fullback Lou Baldacci and halfback Branoff began hammering the Spartan line. Duffy went to an eight-man front, but it could not prevent Branoff from crashing over the goal line behind a Kramer block for a touchdown.

After a few minutes with State unable to move the ball, Duffy had halfback Clarence Peaks quick-kick from his own eighteen. The Green and White smashed into Michigan's Terry Barr, downing him on his own twenty-seven. On the very next play, the Wolverines fumbled, and State had the break for which it had been looking. With the ball on the five, Peaks headed around right end in quest of a score. He met Ron Kramer, and the meeting was not pleasant, as the All-American end flattened Peaks for a 4-yard loss. Morrall then went back to pass, tucked it under his arm, and headed for the goal line. Although it looked as if he would score, Michigan got him at the three and took over on downs.

There was no more scoring that quarter or the next, and the first half ended 7-0. The two marching bands put on a wonderful halftime show, more than worthy of the competitive nature of the game itself. In the third quarter, State got the ball on the Michigan thirty-nine off a hurried Kramer punt. The powerful backfield consisting of Morrall, Peaks, Kowalczyk, and Gerry Planutis drove down to the Wolverine five. This time there was no pass. Morrall snuck twice, down to the one. There Planutis dove over right tackle and the score became 7-7.

The gamebreaker came five minutes later, as the Wolverines swarmed in on Earl Morrall, blocking his punt after he had juggled the snap. From the twenty-one it took Michigan six plays to score, as quarterback Jim Maddock pushed in from the one. As the game ended and their heroes prevailed, the Big House throng chanted "Rose Bowl . . . Rose Bowl . . . Rose Bowl . . ."

"They were tough," said Oosterbaan of State after the game. "We couldn't get out from behind the eight-ball," was the coach's reply as to why his team had not thrown to Kramer once all day. "Their quick kicks and our mistakes kept us back there all the time." But for Daugherty it was a mean defeat. His team had won the statistical battle overall and yet had lost, mainly due to self-inflicted mistakes of which Michigan had taken advantage.

The Spartans headed home for their initial date in East Lansing, against a strong (6-3-1 for the year) Stanford team fresh from beating Ohio State 6-0. The team shook off the ugly Ann Arbor memory and laid the lumber to the Californians to the tune of 38-14. Notre Dame awaited.

The Irish came in ranked #4, Michigan State #13. Ex-GI Gerry Planutis came up big in this confrontation before 52,007 at State. The thundering fullback crashed over with the winning TD, set up with a fumble recovery, and kicked three PATs as Spartans surprised the mighty Irish, 21-7. Planutis, who had been discovered by State recruiters while playing for an army team in Trieste, got plenty of backfield help from the fleet Kowalczyk and Peaks, along with field general Earl Morrall.

Daugherty was now beginning to be noticed. *Sports Illustrated* stated that much of the credit for the big win was owed to this "sturdy, rocklike man of whom the U.S. is bound to hear more." Although State was acknowledged to have the best backfield in the Big Ten, the magazine took special note of his work with the line. "Daugherty is an old lineman himself (Syracuse '40) and his Michigan State line last week, led by guard Embry Robinson, outcharged Notre Dame's forwards all day and turned in a devastating demonstration of downfield blocking. Behind them, with blazing precision, came the backs."

Until then, the larger world had not yet caught on to Duffy's magic. While he kept them laughing, he disguised an incredibly fertile football mind. "My good friend, Duffy Daugherty," wrote Bear Bryant, "is so delightfully witty that some people meeting him for the first time tend to forget that behind his twinkling eyes and hilarious sense of humor lies one of the sharpest minds in football."

Regarding himself as a teacher, coach, and salesman in his technically written 1967 book, *Defense Spartan Style*, Daugherty believed a successful football coach must sell defense. "You must make your players believe that defense is not just a part of the game—it is *the* game. If your opponent cannot score, you cannot lose."

Obviously, he had sold defense to this team. In conference games the Spartans of 1955 cut 10 points off opponents' scoring from the previous season, and 60 yards off the opposition's total offense. In addition, no team scored more than 14 points against Michigan State in 1955, two scored 7, and three did not score at all. Given the absence of big scoring plays recorded against his Spartans, there was already a foreshadowing of Daugherty's later, much more refined thinking, recorded in 1967: knowing a game could get away on a single pass play or a cleverly designed run, he employed a "stay at home" defensive system. "In the old days," explained line coach Lou Agase, "you would line up in that seven-man box and everyone would fire in there. That's all there was to it." It was simple because no one threw the ball and teams did not use mousetrap blocks—plays in which a charging lineman would be taken out from the side without seeing the block coming. Daugherty's defensive scheme had a zone flavor. Defenders, including linemen, stayed at home, protecting their own turf until they were certain where the ball was going. For the always-calculating coach, it was a trade-off. "We expect to give up some ground," he reasoned, "but we're trying to stop the long run, the play that will kill you. Our defense is like elastic—we'll stretch, all right, but we try not to snap." Similarly, the Spartan defensive backs were instructed to assume every play was a pass, again making sure that a running play was indeed running play with the runner beyond the line of scrimmage before committing to going after him.

Against Illinois, Earl Morrall executed a specially rehearsed play, delivering the ball to end Dave Kaiser for a 60-yard score that broke a 7-7 deadlock. Now #5, State went on to a 21-7 win. It was now off to Wisconsin to face a dangerous Badger bunch. The beat went on as Kowalczyk helped power the Spartans to a 27-0 conquest in Camp Randall. One week later, Earl Morrall picked off an errant Purdue lateral and went 90 yards for a TD in another 27-0 rout, this one at West Lafayette. Bigger news, however, came out of Illinois, where the Illini upended #4 Michigan by a decisive 25-6 count. With Ohio State ineligible to return to Pasadena by virtue of the no-repeat rule, Michigan State now controlled its own Rose Bowl destiny in Duffy's second year.

Ranked third nationally, the Spartans pounded visiting Minnesota, 42-14, and followed that with a 33-0 pasting of Marquette, also in East Lansing. Although Ohio State copped the Big Ten title at 6-0, its two non-conference losses put the Buckeyes at 7-2, ranking them four spots behind now #2 Michigan State. The Spartans were heading to the Rose Bowl, 5-1 in the Big Ten and 8-1 overall.

The Spartans ranked 3rd in the Big Ten in total offense and defense. Their scoring margin (16 points per game) was second only to champion Ohio State. The Buckeyes, owing to a pair of nonconference defeats, ranked 5th nationally, according to the pollsters, while the Green and White were second. Walt Kowalczyk was 4th in rushing and second in scoring, Earl Morrall 4th in passing. Kowalczyk averaged 6.7 yards per carry, second among the ground gainers. Morrall joined tackle Norm Masters, a future Packer, on the first-team All–Big Ten (both were consensus All-Americans), while center Carl Nystrom was named to the second unit.

The great Red Sanders coached Michigan State's Rose Bowl opponent, UCLA. The game was a study in contrasts. The proud Sanders ran a single wing (direct snap to his do-everything tailback) offense, while Duffy was awash in complexity. He would use a standard T formation, one with players winged off to the side, perhaps a single wing, and could move behind an unbalanced line (one in which the center is not placed in the center of the seven-man line). Duffy's defenses might be in a 5-4-2 arrangement, only to shift to 6-3-2 at other points.

Interest in the game built in part due to an exchange between the quipping Daugherty and the serious Sanders at a football awards banquet held in New York in early December.

"Duffy, since we get the choice of the ball this year, what kind of football would you like to use?" Sanders inquired.

"It's not going to make much difference to Duffy," cracked Bud Wilkinson, seated between the two. "He's not going to get to use it much anyway."

"We're not going to need it much," remarked Daugherty, always getting the last quip.

Californians did not know what to make of the humorist coach of the Spartans. Not only was he a virtual stand-up comic when he wanted to be, he was totally devoid of the usual coaching paranoia. While his predecessors at the Rose Bowl, like Michigan's Fritz Crisler and Ohio State's Woody Hayes, all but slammed the doors on the media during practices, Duffy invited the public in as well, and then went one step further in the opposite direction: he would take the microphone and explain his team's plays as they ran them.

Daugherty characteristically luxuriated in his own celebrity and that of his team, consenting to a Byzantine social schedule. He accepted invitations from every quarter, held twice-daily press conferences, and played golf just three days before the game. His apparent hubris was unsettling to many, including Sanders. "Daugherty almost acts as though he considers this just a game," said one observer. While the Spartans indulged themselves in the warm California sun, Sanders posted messages on the team black-board, stating, "Remember—between now and January 2—SLEEP is most important!"

What was Duffy up to, one wonders? Was it arrogance? Was it whimsy? Or was he just having fun? The vote here is the latter. But it was also having its effect. It was putting him front and center in Los Angeles, and it was most certainly rattling the taciturn Sanders. Sanders remonstrated daily over the less than healthy status of his star tailback, the mercurial Ronnie Knox, not noting that Duffy was missing several key players as well.

Sanders sounded gloomier by the day. After viewing some State film he moaned, "We're ready for our finest game, but that might not be enough. They might be the finest Michigan State team ever and the finest Big Ten team ever to come to the Rose Bowl." That the finest up to then had been a Michigan squad that left Pasadena with a 49-0 win provided insight into Sanders's mood, as did the coach's practice techniques. Sanders used three men in the deep receiver set, hoping that some good punt returns would obviate State's punting advantage. He also practiced goal-line stands regularly. "We figure we might be in a lot of them."

Conversely, Daugherty relaxed in his Huntington-Sheraton Hotel press conferences virtually up to game time, with beer in hand. "I'm not an optimist. I'm a real-ist," the coach said to those wondering about his seeming overconfidence. "Our boys have been knocked down lots of times but they always get up to make the tackles. And no man in the country with a football is going to run as fast as Walt Kowalczyk without one." Not making the game bigger than life, Daugherty pointed out, "Look, what good would it do me to get out the crying towel? I'm sure Red will come up with something. We know we're in for our toughest game. But we hope we have a great football team."

The game was unforgettable. In a defensive struggle, State led 14-7 with but seven minutes to go, as Daugherty calmly munched his apple—something for which he became famous over the years—on the sidelines. Sanders sent Knox into the contest to perform his wonders. And he did. After a few sputtering plays he fired a 47-yard aerial to Jim Decker on the Spartan seven. By the time UCLA crashed into the end zone, Duffy had tossed his apple, and the score was 14-14 with just four minutes left.

State then started a drive and got down to the Bruin 30 with a minute remaining. Duffy then had Gerry Planutis attempt a field goal, but the ball flew way off to the right. It looked as if the game was over.

Uclan offensive coach Jim Myers was not down for the count. He wanted his team to throw. An official flagged him for an illegal signal from the sideline, however, and walked off 15 yards, pushing the Bruins back to their own five. Now it was Knox's turn never to say die. He unloaded a running pass from the end zone, disappearing under a heap of Spartans as he released the ball. It fell incomplete. Now it looked like the game was over for sure.

But wait! An ineligible receiver had been downfield, so more yards were marched off against UCLA. With 30 seconds left, Knox punted. Clarence Peaks smartly called for a fair catch, only to have a Bruin crash into him, resulting in a 15-yard walkoff against UCLA. From the 31-yard line, Daugherty had end Dave Kaiser try one last field goal. Good! The final was Michigan State 17, UCLA 14.

After the game a bitterly unhappy Sanders was asked which player had given him the most trouble. "The guy who kicked the field goal," he said glumly. In the Michigan State dressing room, Daugherty, the 1955 choice as national Coach of the Year, was busy munching on another apple, accepting congratulations from Biggie Munn, ready to hold court with the press.

A delightful postscript emerged from the victory in Pasadena. The win gave birth to one of Duffy's favorite stories, an anecdote that became a near text for him as the gridiron equivalent of St. Paul's spiritual words to the church at Corinth: "Everyone who competes in the games goes into strict training. They do it to get a crown that will not last, but we do it to get a crown that will last forever. Therefore, I do not run like a man running aimlessly; I do not fight like a man beating the air. No, I beat my body and make it my slave so that after I have preached to others, I myself will not be disqualified for the prize" (1 Corinthians 9:24-27).

In the game, Daugherty noticed something strange as Kaiser booted the game winner. "Nice going, Dave," the coach said as Kaiser came to the sidelines amid the euphoria of his teammates, "but I noticed you didn't watch the ball after you kicked it. How come?"

"You're right, coach," Kaiser replied. "I didn't watch the ball. I was watching the referee to see how he would call it. You see, I forgot my contact lenses. They are back at the hotel. I couldn't even see the goalposts!"

Daugherty was enraged initially but upon reflection took a different view. Kaiser's success was a study in discipline. He had practiced endlessly, and he knew the angle and the distance, even if he couldn't see his target. He had programmed his body to execute properly because he had engaged in discipline, and his discipline paid off.

CHAPTER 5

Celebrity

"Ref, you stink," the coach called out as the official marked off a five-yard penalty. "How do I smell from here, smart aleck?" asked the ref after stepping off fifteen.

—A Duffy favorite he attributed to AP sportswriter Fritz Howell

With twenty-five of thirty-eight MSU lettermen returning, including the estimable Clarence Peaks, Walt Kowalczyk, Dan Currie, and John Matsko, 1956 appeared to hold the potential for a serious run at an undefeated season and the national championship.

Duffy offered guarded optimism. "If we stay physically whole and get our share of breaks, I look for this team to produce a very creditable record," the coach stated carefully. "We have good speed, satisfactory depth at most positions, and fine spirit. There is better size, too, especially among the sophomores."

In reality, the team was loaded. It had size, talent, and depth. The only concern was quarterback, where Earl Morrall had starred for several years and was now heading for a career in the NFL. An untested Pat Wilson would be calling signals for the Spartans.

The season opened with 55,000 Spartan rooters watching the mighty Green and

White subdue a game but overmatched Stanford, 21-7. Duffy had the California team befuddled with his machinations. Rather than lining up in an unbalanced line to the right on the T, wing T, and single-wing formations, the Spartans tilted to the left.

Clearly, Duffy understood image-building well before it became an art if not a science in the marketing-laden United States. Early evidence of this is that the face adorning the cover of the October 8, 1956, edition of *Time* did not belong to Dwight Eisenhower, Adlai Stevenson, or even Richard Nixon in that election year. It belonged to Hugh Daugherty. It is unlikely that Daugherty, as successful as he had become, could have been the cover boy of such a publication were he not a self-promoter, one who had carefully crafted a public persona, that of a "character."

Not that the football world had not revised their estimate of Daugherty's coaching prowess sharply upward after the 1955 season. Other than the award as Coach of the Year, there was no better evidence of this than that mighty Texas offered Duffy a chance to head to the Lone Star State to direct the gridiron fortunes of the Longhorns. Life in East Lansing was fine for Duffy, however, and the Spartan coach suggested Texas might want to consider a friend, Darrell Royal, from the University of Washington, for the job. Daugherty proved as astute a judge of coaching talent as he did of playing prowess, as Royal posted a 167-47-5 record over his twenty-year tenure at Texas, a mark good enough to get him into the College Football Hall of Fame. Five years later Duffy would recommend one of his assistants, Bob Devaney, to Nebraska, where the eventual Hall of Famer and mentor of national champions would register a 101-20-2 mark.

Nonetheless, gridiron success could hardly have been enough for Daugherty. Besides, there were many other successful coaches, mentors that scarcely earned a mention in anything but the sports rags. Moreover, he was far from ragingly successful by early October 1956. His lifetime record stood at 13-7. He had completed one winning and one losing season.

Duffy was on the cover of *Time*, in this era before there were sports information directors, because he had learned at just forty-one years of age how to become "good copy." Described as "cheerfully irreverent" and "a merry man with an Irishman's gregariousness and a leprechaun's smile," the article in *Time* noted his wit. Coming off a Rose Bowl season, Daugherty told *Time*, "I should give a lot of credit for last year's success to my staff. That's only fair." Then, already the master of timing, he added, "I don't see why I shouldn't. I gave them *all* the credit for what happened in 1954."

The article provided a number of glimpses into the essence of Daugherty. Despite his relaxed and mirthful exterior, it noted that he was "one of the hardest driving coaches in the country." Daugherty rarely slept the night *after* a game. "I figure I've done everything I can to prepare the team for the game. But after the game I'm so keyed up I stay up playing it over and over." Indeed, there was very good reason for Daugherty to sleep well the night before the contest, because the article noted how thorough, painstaking, and detail-oriented was his game preparation. Good old "Things will work themselves out" Duffy did not exist. Daugherty was an intensely serious competitor who made his lists and checked them more than twice. In fact, *Time* noted that his "driving attention to detail" was the main and only secret to his system, a film-studying detail orientation that made certain that no player on offense or defense made the same mistake twice.

Far from the clownish buffoon who could recruit but couldn't coach, the coal miner's son was already renowned for the intricate nature of his multiple offense attack. More than that, the man who had been down on his knees in the mines made certain his players were driven to the edge when it came to conditioning. Every workout began with grueling calisthenics, and after several hours of intense drills, the players concluded with a brutal set of wind sprints. During one practice Daugherty complained that the guys were dragging. "I don't know why—maybe it's the weather," he mused. "Now we're going to run you, because that's the only way you'll stay in shape."

The running was brutal. First the players would go full out in 50-yard bursts. "Dig it! Dig it! Dig it!" the coach would holler at his winded players. After Daugherty was satisfied, he sent them in stocking feet to the stadium, where they ran up the concrete stairs to the top of monstrous Spartan Stadium three times.

But Duffy kept it fun. "Growl at 'em!" he would command his linemen. During one smashing blocking drill he told tackle Fran O'Brien, an earnest sophomore, to growl at the defensive lineman. When O'Brien obediently complied, he was hit from the side. "What happened?" he asked a guffawing Daugherty from the bottom of the pile.

"If they pull that on you in a game, Fran, you complain to the referee," said the jolly mentor.

Fun, but rough—violent, even. In scrimmages, Daugherty baited the players. "We're just dying to have some of you show us you're football players," he taunted. "All you have to do is rack somebody up a few times and you'll play plenty for us." The hitting is intense, a player curses, and Duffy steps in quickly. "All right, son, all right," he intoned. "We don't need any sermons this morning." Players banged into one another until they were dizzy. Bells were rung, and pain was a constant reminder of the grim nature of the game.

"You see a guy out on a canoe on Red Cedar River with his girl and a blanket and you wonder what you're doing it for," said kicker/end Dave Kaiser, putting it into perspective, "but other times you get out there feeling good and you just plain want to butt heads."

Under the surface of simplicity, there was nothing simple about Daugherty. In his heavily run-oriented offense ("We are not a passing team"), he ran a single wing, a T and split T, or even a belly series. In the single wing, the back stands in what is currently called a "shotgun" position and runs behind a convoy of blockers. The T is the more conventional style with the quarterback under center (the split T simply makes the ends *wide* receivers). In the belly series, several running backs shoot through the line in near contiguous fashion, leaving the defense to wonder which has the ball, one of the running backs or perhaps the quarterback. As for the quarterback, he might abandon all of the above, fake the ball to a running back, and roll out to the outside on what is called a bootleg. Duffy had his team blocking and running out of thirty-two different formations.

The former lineman minimized the intellectual demands on his backs. "Backs feel like they're fooling people. They don't mind running through plays. Teaching them is easy." It was the linemen who needed to do the skull work. The challenge was to get quick movement and automatic, yet correct, execution. "The worst thing that can happen to offensive football," Daugherty lectured, "is indecision." Therefore, a premium was placed on getting the interior linemen to reach a level of functioning such that, even in the late and exhaustive phases of a game, they would operate correctly among the seventy-two different plays. Daugherty sagely reduced the intellectual burden on his linemen by having them master twenty-five different principles, applicable across the entire spectrum of plays.

Duffy was proud of his sophisticated offense, his stay-at-home defense, and especially his acumen at making prudent adjustments. "Last year," he stated, "after our halftime talks, State scored 87 points in the third quarter. Our opponents scored seven."

Fresh from *Time* fame, Daugherty and his charges faced a powerful Michigan bunch, one that had decimated UCLA 47-0 in their opener. Daugherty put together an offensive game plan that was simple. "We hope to spread out the defense by splitting our linemen," he explained, "and then run up the middle." He did exactly that, using the forceful Peaks/Kowalczyk duo. On defense, the ingenious Daugherty had a surprise or two for the opponents. He showed a seven-man front but would have two defenders float back as linebackers. To quell long passes, the coach employed his "umbrella" defense in which two interior safety men were bordered in an arc arrangement by two defensive halfbacks. The Wolverines did not put up 47 before a throng of 101,001 on this soggy, intermittent rainstorm day at Michigan Stadium. In "the hardest fought game I've ever seen," according to Daugherty, State prevailed 9-0.

Neither side scored in the first half of bitter combat. Then, early in the second half, linebacker Archie Matsos picked off a jump pass for the Spartans with a single hand. Nine plays later, kicker and captain John Matsko delivered successfully from the twenty-one, and it was State 3, Michigan 0. In the fourth quarter, a forced Wolverine fumble was followed by a Dennis Mendyk smash over right tackle to lock up the win.

Life could scarcely be better on the banks of the Red Cedar River, and Daugherty was sucking all the juices out of the experience. He had a radio show and two weekly TV gigs, in addition to a host of speaking opportunities, few of which he turned down. Gerald Holland of *Sports Illustrated* caught up with the genial mentor as he and the campus prepared for the season's first home game, against the hapless Indiana Hoosiers. Duffy was hurriedly trying to find a parking place. He was close to being late for the pep rally on this magical evening. Eventually Daugherty settled on parking in a driveway behind another car. He left his keys in his vehicle, should it be in the way. From there he made his way over to the rally. After the "MSU Fight Song" the student master of ceremonies noticed the coach and roared, "And here's the man we've been waiting for—Coach Duffy Daugherty." On cue the truly Big Man on Campus headed for the stage, winking at his soon-to-be-introduced players off to the side. So much of Duffy's national prominence owed to what was going on at the rally. Daugherty had managed to transform the image of the big-time college football coach from that of uptight "one game at a time" purveyor of footballspeak to that of entertainer as well as winner.

Basking in the crowd's adoration, the up-from-Barnesboro Daugherty finally put up a hand to stop the cheering and said, "Well, I hope we have another nice sunshiny day tomorrow." Then with exquisite timing added, "Like last Saturday," referring to the monsoon in Ann Arbor in which the Spartans triumphed.

With the assembled multitude howling, the coach added, "Oh, yes, somebody did tell me it sprinkled a little. I guess I didn't notice."

After a student hammered a large drum for effect, Duffy began customizing his address further for the partisan crowd. "Well, it will certainly be wonderful to play on our home field for the first time this year. We're kind of a road team this year and of course the boys got a kick out of going to California, but they were saying this afternoon there's no thrill like playing before your own crowd, your own fellow students. They were saying today that there's no spirit like the Spartan spirit and they'll certainly be giving everything out there tomorrow."

Although they were outscored 47-6 in their first two games, Duffy found a way to present the Hoosiers as a worthy opponent. Several players then spoke. For Duffy, however, the pep rally was not the last of his appearances so close to the game. He made a speech at a press dinner, then did an off-the-cuff installment of his fifteen-minute radio show, with Indiana coach Bernie Crimmins and Baltimore Colts executive Keith Molesworth as guests.

At the end of the show Daugherty turned to Crimmins and said, "Bernie, I understand my sponsors (a Lansing automobile dealer) placed a new car at your disposal while you're in town. How do you like it?"

"Duffy, it's a beauty," chimed in a cooperative Crimmins. "In fact, I've just about decided that I'll get one like it when I get home."

"That's fine, I drive one myself and I think they're great," said the natural ham from Barnesboro. "Say, Bernie, I didn't intend this to be a commercial. The announcer does that. I was just curious, that's all."

"Sure, Duff," Crimmins hit back on cue with wink of his eye.

It wasn't over for Duffy just yet, however. It was time to head over to the ballroom stage of the Hotel Olds in Lansing to address alumni on this homecoming weekend. He sagely praised his staff and claimed, "They do all the work. I just kind of walk around."

Duffy used fifty players as his multiple offense generated a 53-6 blowout of Indiana in East Lansing. Duffy felt bad for Indiana. "I don't like to see the score go that high, but there was nothing I could do about it," he said chomping on his apple.

The now undefeated (3-0) Spartan coach, with his team regaled as the best in the land by the pollsters, pressed on through the weekend nonstop. He spoke at an alumni dinner, entertained some visiting relatives, did his Detroit-based WJIM-TV show off the seat of his pants, and managed to review the film of the Indiana game with his staff. The following week his team would be headed for Notre Dame to face an Irish squad destined to lose eight of its ten games.

Physically, the team was in pretty good shape, according to Duffy. Peaks was in excellent health, star guard Pat Burke had emerged from the Hoosier confrontation with little more than a charley horse, injured Dave Kaiser might be ready to return to action, and Walt Kowalczyk—well, he was "limping much better."

Duffy was concerned about his team's psychological readiness. "You fellows have got to remember that you can never take Notre Dame for granted," he cautioned his troops. "One of these Saturdays they're going to be one of the best teams in the country, and I just hope it's not this Saturday. You've got to remember that you won't only be playing Hornung and Aubrey Lewis, you'll be playing Rockne and George Gipp and the Four Horsemen."

He then looked over at Clarence Peaks. "Clarence, what would you do if Rockne tackled you Saturday?"

"I believe that I'd just leave the stadium," replied the bewildered Peaks.

Depending on the oddsmaker, the Spartans were two- to three-touchdown favorites in South Bend. At the team meeting, the Notre Dame–Purdue film was shown, with much coaching commentary from Duffy and his staff. At its conclusion, Daugherty walked to the front of the room and sat on the table facing his team. "This team doesn't need any pep talk. You're good and you're going to win," he told them. "When you're in scoring position they'll set up that chant and you may not be able to hear the signals. If that happens, you ask the referee for an official timeout until you can hear the signals clearly."

Perhaps the team did need a pep talk. The Spartans were flat.

Notre Dame was not. The Irish had decided to wake up the echoes by inviting all the past Notre Dame All-Americans to the game. During the Friday workout the State players watched with awe as a number of Irish legends—including the Four Horsemen, Johnny Lujack, Angelo Bertelli, and Leon Hart—surrounded the practice field. The following morning, Coach Daugherty decided to offer one of his better jokes to the team. There was scarcely a laugh. He then lit into them, charging them with not being focused and being ripe for a season-destroying upset.

There are few events bigger than major college football in South Bend. At noon, the Spartans entered the two chartered buses that would take them from nearby Elkhart to Notre Dame Stadium for the confrontation. With everyone, the team, Biggie Munn, the dean of students, the squad cars, and the motorcycles of the Indiana State Police ready, only one person was missing—Duffy Daugherty. Daugherty was back in the lobby of the hotel on his hands and knees peering into the face of a Bedlington terrier.

"What's his name?" the coach asked the girl with the dog.

"Baa-Baa."

"Baa-Baa," Daugherty addressed the dog. He later recalled, "I said, 'Give me your left paw.' That's your right paw." The dog offered the left paw.

The Michigan State business manager, a nervous Lyman Frimodig, was now in the lobby witnessing this interaction.

"All set and ready to go, Duff," he said, partly to inform the coach and partly to direct him to the bus.

Ignoring the air of urgency, Duffy looked at Frimodig. "I used to be a dog trainer, watch this," he said, using his arms to form a hoop.

"Jump!" he commanded Baa-Baa.

Baa-Baa merely presented his right paw. "You see, Frim, the first requisite for a dog trainer is that he has to know more than the dog."

Patting the dog's head, Daugherty concluded, "And that is why I gave up dog training."

A few hours later, a conservatively attired Daugherty was ready for the kickoff, with an Irish shillelagh under his arm. The homecoming queen had presented it to Daugherty in 1954, but when Notre Dame won the game, he had given it to Terry Brennan. The Irish coach gave it back after the Spartan win in 1955.

Notre Dame's quarterback, Paul Hornung, soon to win the Heisman Trophy, also smelled an upset. In the huddle, he told the squad, "Listen, you guys, if we can stay fired up, this team can be had."

The game was a killer. Duffy could feel the tension. He tossed the shillelagh to a player on the bench and donned a pair of sunglasses to accommodate the brightness of the afternoon. Off went the suit coat soon after, and Duffy became more animated, crouching, prowling the sidelines, and talking on the phones with his assistants in the booth upstairs.

After a scoreless first period, Hornung threw a few strikes and got the Irish down to the Spartan eight. A few plays later, Frank Reynolds took a Hornung pitchout and scored, after which Hornung converted and it was 7-0. Dennis Mendyk took the kickoff to midfield before Hornung nailed the 183-pounder. A dozen plays later the Green and White scored. Notre Dame then moved down the field quickly. It was only because the great Clarence Peaks had picked off a Notre Dame pass in the end zone that the Irish did not garner a 14-7 advantage. In any case, Peaks had run the ball out to the twenty-two, only to have a clipping infraction push the Spartans back to their own seven. The rankled coach ordered some line plunges to run out the half. On the first play, however, Peaks navigated through a host of Irish defenders and raced 93 yards for a score. At least it looked like a score. It was called back for clipping. In the ensuing punt attempt, the snap was botched and Notre Dame took over in the Spartan kitchen. The time mercifully ran out before the Irish could score.

Although the score was even at 7-7, the atmosphere in the respective locker rooms at halftime was very different. Irish mentor Terry Brennan was jubilant. "Fellows," he intoned, "you have 30 minutes more to pull off one of Notre Dame's greatest achievements."

Duffy was angry. He asked his center what had happened on the ill-fated snap. "It was as if someone had his hands on that football," was the reply.

"Don't bring the supernatural into this thing," Duffy claims to have said.

"Hey, maybe it was old George Gipp reaching up to put his hand on the football," chimed Don Berger.

"Don't be sacrilegious," said Duffy. "Maybe it was George Gipp reaching *down*."

The spell was broken, and mirth was the order of the day for the man who always found a way to have fun. Daugherty pulled his team in a circle and encouraged them to tell any joke they wanted. The final joke took so long the chuckling players barely got out on the field in time. The second half belonged to Michigan State, with a final score of 47-14.

As the game ended, Daugherty returned to the conservative outfit he had worn at the outset of the afternoon and, with shillelagh in hand, greeted his friend Brennan warmly.

The high lasted exactly one week. The seemingly almighty Spartans then headed to Illinois, where a grossly inferior Illini team (that would finish a puny 2-5-2), with its coach, Ray Eliot, being openly scorned with "Goodbye Ray" signs. Husky halfback Abe Woodson, who barely missed making the Olympic team as a hurdler, took off down the field for what appeared to be the winning touchdown. With one Spartan defender in his way, Woodson did what he did best, hurdling the defender as 71,119 homecoming fans cheered his 82-yard sprint into the end zone. Minutes before, with the Illini down 13-6, Woodson had ripped 70 yards to tie the score. In all he scored three TDs and rolled up 198 yards against the #1 team in the nation, en route to a stunning 20-13 upset.

As for the Spartans, there was more to the story than a lack of passion. The played the Illini shorthanded. The two Spartan ends, Dave Kaiser and Bob Jewett, were out of the game, along with tackle Pat Burke, who had been nicked up against Notre Dame. The great Walt Kowalczyk was injured at the start of the season. If that were not bad enough, with the team up 13-0, Clarence Peaks stepped in a hole, tore a cartilage, and was gone for the season.

"They deserved to win," said a disappointed Daugherty. "They played inspired, determined football."

The loss to Illinois was a killer. It ruined what appeared to be a perfect season and a national championship, something that would put Daugherty at the same level as his football mentor, Clarence "Biggie" Munn, who had turned the trick in 1952. The impact of the loss was felt for the rest of the season.

Although the Spartans shredded Wisconsin 33-0 at home immediately after the loss to Illinois, they barely got out alive the following week, winning 12-9 at home to a Purdue team playing without ace quarterback Lenny Dawson. A week after that the Spartans headed for Minneapolis to face the 5-1-1 Golden Gophers. After having been thoroughly outplayed by the Boilermakers in the 12-9 struggle, the Green and White battled the Gophers evenly, gaining 333 yards to Minnesota's 324. The score was almost but not quite even, however, as Minnesota won 14-13, with the difference being the play of quarterback Bobby Cox.

Now 6-2, the team had one game left, against a weak 3-6 Kansas State squad. The Spartans rolled 38-17 despite a dozen fumbles, making the triumph less than an artistic delight.

Despite the two disappointing losses, Michigan State closed the season 7-2, and ranked #9 nationally. At 4-2 in the Big Ten, the Spartans finished a single game behind champion Iowa, and a half game in arrears of Michigan (5-2) and Minnesota (4-1-2). State was the top team in the league on offense, 3rd on defense. Moreover, their fourteen-point average margin (22 to 8.2 points per game) was by far the best in the conference. No other team had a margin larger than seven. It was, as they say, a team effort. Despite ranking 2nd in rushing, no Spartan ranked among the top dozen ground gainers. In addition, State was shut out of the All–Big Ten first team. Tackle Joel Jones, guard Dan Currie, and center John Matsko made the second squad.

It had been an injury-marred season, with the likes of Kowalczyk, Pat Burke, and Dave Kaiser down much of the time. Nonetheless, the Spartans had turned in a strong 7-2 season, and on the strength of the experience some of the reserves had gotten in this campaign, they had reason to hope that the Green and White could reap a strong harvest in 1957.

Almost

"With a legion of lettermen returning we should have a great season if the coaches come through."

—Duffy on his team's prospects for 1957

By 1956 things became more tense between Munn and Daugherty. As certainly as Duffy did not walk through Munn's "open door" during a troubled 1954 because he didn't want to, he stayed away in 1955 because he didn't need to. Watching Daugherty supplant him in celebrity had to burn deeply within the proud Biggie Munn. Gerald Holland of *Sports Illustrated*, in a 1962 feature on Munn, captured the man's expansive ego. While sitting in his office Munn noted some of this achievements. "These four citations here," he said to Holland, pointing: "All-America guard in 1931, unanimous choice; Christy Walsh's 25-year All-America covering the years 1924–1948; Coach of the Year, 1952; National Football Hall of Fame, 1959. Now the point is, the point is that no other man—living or dead—has all these citations."

Thumbing through the *Michigan State Facts Book*, Munn mentioned a few other of his accomplishments. "Plus, all sorts of other honors. Captain of Minnesota, 1931; unanimous choice for All–Big Ten; winner of the *Chicago Tribune*'s award as the Big

Ten's most valuable player; elected to *Sports Illustrated*'s first Silver Anniversary All-America in 1956." Munn was understandably proud of his achievements, as he was the definition of the self-made man by 1950s standards. As an eight-year-old in Grow Township, Minnesota, young Clarence Munn lost his father and observed his mother going out to support the family. He had always worked. At Minnesota, he worked four hours a day, received no athletic scholarship, nor any help from alumni. From an anonymous childhood in rural Minnesota, Munn had emerged as a Goliath, one who was both respected and loved. Sensitive to causes, Munn had given his energies to the Boy Scouts of America, blood drives, the Red Cross, the US Olympic Committee, and the Fellowship of Christian Athletes. Testimonials adorned his office, typified by a statement from a sportswriter. "Biggie Munn," wrote George S. Alderton, sports editor of the *Lansing State Journal*, "is the greatest man I have ever met."

Munn was an eloquent defender of intercollegiate athletics, particularly football. "When a football player or any athlete walks out on the field, he usually has a number on his back," the broad-shouldered, 230-pound Munn stated to Holland. "That alone identifies him. The people who have paid to see the game will judge him entirely by what he does. And what he does is out in the open for everyone to see. The player cannot hide behind anybody. His creed or color, what side of the tracks he was born on, how much money he has in the bank, his political affiliations—none of these things are involved. He is on his own. He cannot lean on anybody.

"I have always admired the boy who is willing to take part in a rough, combative game like football. This is competition of the highest order. It is true that not everybody is equipped for this kind of competition. Other people may take part in other activities—music, drama, debating, and so on. They are not criticized for doing so. On the contrary, they are usually complimented. But sometimes those who are unable to take part in a physical contest resent the boys who do. They resent the crowds that cheer the athletes; they resent the publicity the boys receive. Well, publicity works two ways. It can build a man up; it can tear a man down. I know this all too well from my own experience."

For Munn, college football had a unique place in the university. "It brings the alumni back to the university and draws everyone closer together. I cannot imagine Michigan State without its football team. It would not be the same place. You cannot tell me that the University of Chicago is what it used to be in the days of Alonzo Stagg."

As for scholarships, Munn was quick to the defense. "The boys who play football at Michigan State are not hired entertainers. They are *students*. They must meet the academic requirements that are set up by the Big Ten. They must compete in the classroom as well as on the athletic field. They live and work and study as part of the student body. They are not isolated in dormitories of their own. Now, I see no reason why these boys should not receive some help in return for their ability to play football. Scholarships are given for music, chemistry, the sciences, and so on. It seems only fair to me."

For Clarence "Biggie" Munn it was all about effort. He would note his favorite maxim above his autograph when signing his book, *Michigan State's Multiple Offense*: The difference between good and great is just little extra effort. It seems it was taking much more than a little extra effort for Munn and Daugherty to get along after the 1955 season. Daugherty apparently resented Munn's "Big Daddy" attitude, one designed to keep Duffy in the shadows. For Munn, however, the sun was shining on Daugherty. He had been Coach of the Year, a Rose Bowl victor, a cover boy on *Time* magazine, featured extensively in *Sports Illustrated*, and regarded as a man of extraordinary wit and verve. All this while Munn built the sports infrastructure at State, one including intramural as well as intercollegiate athletics, out of the public eye.

Their wrangling became open. Duffy would express a desire to take four assistants on a trip, only to have Biggie flex his authoritarian muscle and arbitrarily decree that three assistants would suffice. Things became so unwieldy that President Hannah appointed one Harold B. Tukey, chair of the horticultural department, to arbitrate their differences. Dr. Tukey got nowhere and punted, so to speak. An unhappy Hannah then urged Tukey to reconsider, and met with the two combatants himself, telling them that any more public quarreling would spell the dismissal of one or both of them.

As for the 1957 Spartans, the outlook was very bright. Daugherty's charges were coming off a 16-3 record over the past two campaigns and were returning twenty-eight of forty lettermen from 1956. The complex multiple offense would continue. "We'll make some changes, retaining the plays that have been successful, adding new ones and throwing out some we didn't gain with," Daugherty said in preseason. "On some plays we'll change the blocking to see if that will help." The personnel was very solid. "We've got a good number of veterans returning, including some like Walt Kowalczyk, Dave Kaiser, and Pat Burke, who were injured last year and didn't get to play much." Dan Currie was emerging as the team's center. "We've got a real center," said the coach, "but he has a knee injury and we don't know how much he'll be able to play for us. And we have a couple of good guards so we can afford to try Currie at

CHAPTER SIX

center." Although Peaks was gone, the Spartans had a 190-pound junior speedster named Blanche Martin ready to step in, and at quarterback Jim Ninowski looked as if he might become a Spartan star.

The season opened at home against a pathetic Indiana team, one the Spartans had demolished 53-6 a season ago. This time it was even worse. Michigan State used sixty-seven players in the "contest," but even the third and fourth stringers could not contain the scoring in what became a 54-0 embarrassment.

A trip to Berkeley, California, was next. There, the ground-oriented Spartans surprised the Golden Bears with three TDs and 196 yards in the air in a comfortable 19-0 win.

A week later it was off to Ann Arbor, where Michigan State put on a football clinic, destroying the rival Wolverines 35-6. After hammering through the Michigan line for a score, the Green and White shredded the Wolverine pass defense for two more TDs. Walt Kowalczyk and Jim Ninowski were outstanding as the Spartans awed a crowd of 101,001.

Having not only routed the #6 Wolverines but also administered the worst whipping the Ann Arbor squad had endured in twenty-two years, Michigan State was now being mentioned in the same sentence as seemingly unbeatable Oklahoma. Life was very good if your name was Duffy Daugherty, and playing for the coach was fun. At practices Daugherty would often walk around from group to group, permitting his assistants to do the real coaching. He never took himself too seriously during those winning years. He might point out with annoyance that the backs were running a given play improperly, only to have the quarterback quietly inform him that it was not the play the coach thought it was.

"Can't you take a joke?" the coach would fire back, making a quick recovery.

Off he might go to another group working against the freshmen. "Here's a play that will go all the way!" he might announce with excitement in the huddle.

When it resulted in an interception and a TD runback, Duffy was ready with the first word. "What did I tell you? It went all the way, didn't it? You'll notice I didn't say which way."

If Francie brought their children Danny and Dree to practice, the proud father might walk over and scuffle with Danny and muss up his daughter's hair. Daugherty could not resist comic relief in the grimmest of situations. During one vicious preseason scrimmage in which the coach was urging his charges to hit, he walked over to Dree, looked at her little hand, and suddenly shrieked, "Francie! Dree has a *splinter*!"

Just below the mirthful surface, however, everything was being recorded in Daugherty's extraordinarily fertile brain. Knowing that the game of winning football was in the details, he could reconstruct the entire practice for his staff and team in meetings later on.

Having vanquished Indiana, California, and Michigan by a combined score of 108-6, the Spartans played host to a winless Purdue team. With MSU up 7-0, the Spartans scored what appeared to be a second six-pointer, only to have the score nullified by a penalty. Even worse, at the half State was informed that the callback was incorrect. The infraction was a dead-ball foul, so it should have been assessed on the ensuing kickoff, *after the touchdown*. Though small consolation, Daugherty appreciated the official's honesty and graciously did not inform the press of the admission.

Although Duffy did not realize it at the time, the call would prove crucial. MSU, suffering a letdown, lost its first five fumbles of the season, and only Kowalczyk proved able to penetrate the prepared Boilermaker defense. He ran for 72 yards and a TD, in a shocking 20-13 loss to the visitors, a defeat that may well have cost Daugherty the national as well as Big Ten championships.

The team rebounded a bit, beating a 2-2 Illinois team in a come-from-behind 19-14 verdict before 64,353 at State. The Spartans ran their record to 5-1 a week later, downing Wisconsin 21-7 at Madison.

Duffy was a high-energy man, as chronicled for *Sports Illustrated* by Gerald Holland in 1956. One evening he would be in Detroit addressing the Michigan State Alumni Club, on another he would get three of his players to help with one of his TV shows. He found a way to get to his office each day and cram in an occasional haircut or other personal essential.

The next game was against Notre Dame, always a huge game for the Spartans. Whereas most coaches would be hunkered down in their office looking at film and filling yellow legal pads with gridiron ideas, Duffy wasn't going to fail to smell the roses of big-time football celebrity. The previous year, one in which the Spartans had to travel to South Bend, Duffy had spent one of the evenings on a hayride, originating at the Rowe Ranch outside Lansing. Far from feeling that it would interfere with preparation, the coach was delighted to go on this jaunt planned by the wives of his assistants. A party of fifty, including the Munns, rode on the two wagons, with Duffy singing heartily the barbershop tunes led by assistant Doug Weaver and his harmonica.

When the wagons made it back to the ranch, a jukebox barn dance ensued, with jitterbugging taking center stage. Duffy swilled a beer and watched with joy the antics of basketball coach Forddy Anderson, who, wearing a cap pulled over his ears, was rendering a jitterbug solo. The cap was then passed around, inviting other participants to cut a bit of the barn floor rug as well. Many scooted outside to avoid possible embarrassment, but not Duffy. When he got the cap the coach did a creative dance of his own, much to the amusement of the clapping onlookers.

"You'd think we're playing the Little Sisters of the Poor Saturday!" a voice boomed out. Duffy knew who he was playing, but there was more to life for Daugherty than obsessive preparation for what was then a second-rate opponent. On Wednesday of that week the coach addressed the Downtown Coaches, a collection of Lansing businessmen. The next day he taped his radio show, which would air while he was in South Bend.

When the Spartans reached Elkhart, Indiana, on Friday by their two chartered planes, Duffy was swimming in speaking invitations. Not surprisingly he said he would accept as many as possible. The night before the game he ate dinner with his team and then made an appearance at the Notre Dame press dinner. He kibitzed with Notre Dame coach Terry Brennan, telling him he had brought the Irish shillelagh that had come to symbolize the rivalry.

Even after two dinner meetings the night was not over for the forty-one-year-old Daugherty. He moved upstairs to still another banquet, this one for the local Michigan State alumni. After doing a bit of Duffy stand-up, much to the delight of the partisans, the coach excused himself. He had a date to speak at a Knights of Columbus smoker some distance away.

There was a full house awaiting Duffy, and he loved it. He offered the usually politically correct remarks of respect for Brennan and the morrow's opponent, stating disingenuously that he would be happy to escape with a one-point win. With the crowd now totally nibbling from his hand, Daugherty told one of his favorite and almost certainly apocryphal stories. He would warm the work-ethic Midwestern audience by making the setting the Pennsylvania coal mine in which he had worked with a friend named Fred.

There he would claim that he and Fred would talk of their life dreams—Daugherty's was a college education, and Fred's was to own a tailor-made suit. "Fred talked through his nose," Duffy related, employing a nasal tone, "but he didn't say anything about having his adenoids out. What he wanted most of all was a tailor-made suit." With the audience now firmly within his grip, Daugherty moved the yarn from a heart-warming tale to one of uproarious humor.

"A couple of years ago I went back to Barnesboro," he told the attentive throng. "I got a wonderful welcome home. They put on a Duffy Daugherty night and gave me a dinner. But what I wanted to find out more than anything else was what had happened to Fred. I had realized my dream of going to college, but what about Fred? Did he ever get that tailor-made suit?

Now summoning up a near tearful concern for Fred, he pressed on. "Yes, Fred had realized his dream. After years of backbreaking labor in the mines, he had saved up $300 and taken it to Adam Adamosky, the town tailor. 'Adam,' he said, 'I want you to make me the best tailor-made suit in town.'"

Daugherty then embellished the yarn with detail. Adam had told Fred the time was perfect, he had just gotten in the finest material and had time to make Fred's suit to perfection. After many fittings and adjustments, the suit was done. Fred put it on and strutted down Main Street, bursting with pride. At the corner he encountered Miles Ranck, the editor of the *Barnesboro Star*, who told Fred that he looked fine in the suit, but that there was one slight imperfection: the left sleeve was a tad short.

Of course Fred rushed back to Adam's shop and informed him of the problem. Adamosky comforted his customer, telling him that the seeming imperfection owed to the incredibly high-quality material of which the suit was made, and that all Fred need do was to pull at the sleeve consistently and in several days he would have the finest suit in not just Cambria County but all of Western Pennsylvania.

Duffy, now becoming Fred, yanking at the sleeve, mimicked his friend as he went for another walking tour. When he met some friends, they admired the suit but informed Fred that one of the lapels was sticking up. After hastening back to Adam, Fred was assured by the tailor that by holding his chin on the lapel, he could make the suit perfect within a week. Back on the street, Fred—played to the hilt by Duffy—continued to garner compliments, all the while tugging at the sleeve and holding his chin on the lapel. There was, however, one additional criticism: the pants were a bit full in the seat.

Adam remained calm, instructing Fred to clutch the seat of his pants for a week and all would be perfect. Back on Main Street Fred walked proudly, tugging on his sleeve, holding his chin on the lapel, and grasping the seat of his pants, as two strangers passed.

"What's the matter with that poor guy?" one asked the other. "I don't know," said the friend, "but that's certainly a nice-looking suit."

With the crowd screaming with laughter, Daugherty waved to the adoring mob and slipped out a side door to a car that would return him to Elkhart.

Fortunately for Duffy, the result in 1957 was a near mirror of the 1956 triumph in South Bend, as State pummeled the visiting Irish 34-6 before 75,391 happy rooters in East Lansing.

Now rolling at 6-1 and still in the Rose Bowl picture, the Spartans looked forward to delivering some payback to visiting Minnesota the following week. They did just that, pounding the 4-3 Gophers 42-13. There would be no Pasadena trip in the offing, however, as Ohio State clinched a Rose Bowl berth on the strength of a 17-13 win over a 6-0-1 Iowa squad in Columbus. The big news, however, emanated from South Bend, where the Irish upset the seemingly omnipotent Oklahoma Sooners 7-0, ending their forty-seven-game winning streak.

Although they set a new school fumbling record—thirteen—the Spartans took care of the ball for the last nine and half minutes, ringing up 21 points to beat a 3-5-1 Kansas State team 27-9 in the season finale before just 35,989 in East Lansing.

Depending upon one's point of view, it was either a wonderful season or a bitterly disappointing one. On the plus side, the team went 8-1, equaling the regular season mark just two years previous. On the minus end, the 8-1 mark could just as easily been 9-0, and the #3 national ranking #1 were it not for that 20-13 Purdue debacle. In fairness to the Boilermakers, Purdue won five of its last six games, losing only 20-7 at Ohio State. Nonetheless, they were a beatable team, and the Green and White had them in Red Cedar River country.

Especially galling was that the Spartans had the best offense and defense in the Big Ten. Their meager 182 yards per game (only 57 passing) defensive mark was nearly 40 yards per game stingier than #2 Iowa. They outgained opponents by better than 190 yards per game, far and away the best in the conference.

Kowalczyk finished 5th in rushing (3rd in scoring), Blanche Martin ninth. Martin was a solid all-around performer, ranking 2nd in both punting and punt returns. Jim Ninowski was 4th in passing, and his favorite receiver, Kaiser, was 2nd. Six Spartans—Kowalczyk, Ninowski, center Dan Currie, guard Ellison Kelly, tackle Pat Burke, and end Sammy Williams—were first-team All–Big Ten. Kaiser made the second team.

Despite the disappointment, Duffy Daugherty was no one's subordinate around Michigan State. He was treated as a colleague by the president and had his own identity apart from Biggie Munn. Duffy Daugherty was now his own man.

CHAPTER 7

Off the Radar Screen

"Yes, George was small, but he was slow."

—Daugherty's sarcastic summation of one of Biggie Munn's favorite players

D uffy Daugherty was a winner. Although Ohio State had been dominating the conference, Daugherty's 14-4 Big Ten record over the past three seasons was a solid second, and his overall three-year mark of 24-4 exceeded even that of the Buckeyes. Perhaps more impressive, he had one national Coach of the Year award, one *Time* magazine cover, and one *Sports Illustrated* feature on his résumé. By 1958 Duffy Daugherty had it all. He was smart, funny, and very successful, and in an era in which coaches were technicians, he was way ahead of his time: he was very good copy—a celebrity.

The harvest of success in college football is high expectations. As the 1958 season approached, many felt that the Green and White were the chief obstacles to Ohio State's repeating as league champions. Having had the Big Ten's strongest offensive and defensive team in 1957, the Spartans would have to slip a long way not to be contenders, especially with twenty-four of forty-four lettermen returning. Gone were Walt Kowalczyk, Jim Ninowski, Dan Currie, and Dave Kaiser, among others. Nonetheless, the team did have preseason All-American end Sam Williams and fullback Bob Bereich, along with halfbacks Art Johnson and Dean Look.

The past few seasons did raise a concern, however: a tendency toward up-and-down play. With the brownout against Purdue very fresh in many fans' minds, some felt the team reflected Daugherty's mercurial personality to a fault—dynamic and brilliant much of the time, but given to skidding into the dumps at others. In brief, it seemed that each season the team would throw in at least one gridiron clunker, a loss that would exact substantial pain.

Daugherty did seem to love the psychological combat inherent in coaching a game as emotional as football. He always looked for an edge, knowing how mental the game was. He was amused by one of the intimidating tactics Michigan great Fritz Crisler employed at Michigan Stadium. With the locker rooms of the respective teams directly across from one another, Crisler would leave the door to the Michigan locker room open a crack so he would know when the opposition would leave to head on to the field. He would pause until his opponents were about half out on the field with still another sizable portion slowly making their way out of the locker room. He would then release his Wolverines, who would charge out of their dressing hollering maniacally as they rushed past the walking opponents out onto the field to the cheers of the adoring crowd.

Duffy was not above a gag to fire up his charges. Once in the late 1950s, the team was about to face Michigan but was uncharacteristically flat. Duffy, aware that it was public knowledge that one of his married linemen had been observed pilfering a large box of cereal out of the dormitory, contacted his friend, Sheriff Bill Barnes. Together they hatched a prank.

The following day, the sheriff, with his siren howling and his lights flashing, roared onto the practice field. The drama of the moment startled players and coaches alike. "I'm here to pick up one of your players, coach," Barnes announced sternly. He said he had a warrant for the player's arrest. An indignant assistant rushed at the officer, and pushing and shoving ensued. By the time Daugherty had blown his whistle to restore order, almost every member of the team was ready to fight.

"You can't take him now," the coach begged Barnes. "This is the week of the Michigan game. If you'll just release him to my custody until Saturday's game, we'll see what we can do to get this mess straightened around. I'll see to it that he behaves and doesn't leave town, and I'll turn him over to you after the game."

Sheriff Barnes then made a most generous offer.

"I'll go you one better, coach," he replied. "If you pound Michigan, I'll drop the charges."

The team won handily, and Barnes did not pursue the ruse any further.

One of Daugherty's favorite capers involved Woody Hayes. The grumpy Ohio State mentor once closed practice to Big Ten Skywriters on their visit to Columbus, claiming that he didn't want any outsiders hearing him chew out his players, and he certainly didn't want his words reprinted in the press. When the writers made their trek to Michigan, the impish Daugherty was all set. He too locked the gates to practice, but only for five minutes. "I kept you guys out because I wanted to praise my players, and I didn't want to do it in front of strangers," he cracked, much to the amusement of the scribes. In another Skywriters caper, the coach held court around an outdoor pool. With a straight face, Daugherty went into painstaking detail about the advanced scouting methods and other intricacies of the State football program. He then took one of the youngsters working around the pool and asked him if he knew what the item was that Duffy was holding—a football. Yes, the lad said, he had seen it a time or two. Daugherty then lectured on the aerodynamics of a thrown football, culminating his remarks by directing the youth to go to the far end of the pool. Daugherty then threw the ball toward the young man, who with appropriate nonchalance speared the pigskin with a single hand.

"There you see it, gentlemen," the coach chortled, "pure, coaching genius."

Perhaps it was, but Daugherty neglected identify the young man as Ernie Clark, one of the finest ends Duffy had ever coached.

The 1958 season revealed a fissure in Daugherty's relationship with Athletic Director Munn. The defeats created Munn and Daugherty factions, and the coach felt a contributing factor was that amid reports that Munn wanted to take over the athletic directorship at Minnesota, the Spartans laid a giant 39-12 egg for the Gophers to devour. Clearly Munn had been embarrassed in the eyes of his prospective employers, as he had reportedly complained of the shame associated with building a football structure only to see it crumble before his very eyes.

The breach was serious enough for Hannah to step in and remind both that the university's interests needed to take precedence over their egos. Even that could not have been altogether settling to Munn, who disliked Daugherty's arrangement legitimizing his going directly to the president whenever he was in a stalemate with Munn.

It was an eminently forgettable year for Michigan State football in the Big Ten. The Spartans were the only winless team in the league, despite ranking 2nd in total defensive yardage. Their −5 in turnover margin hurt. Athletic Dean Look led the league in punt returning (32.5 yards per return) and finished 2nd in punting. Williams and Kelly repeated on the All–Big Ten first team, with halfback Look on the second.

The 3-5-1 pill was a difficult tablet for the perpetually optimistic coach to swallow. In retrospect, Daugherty felt he may have been his own worst foe. "I was always tremendously optimistic about the Spartans' chances," he recalled in his autobiography. "I just couldn't help myself. After all, I had recruited these fine young men and I thought always that they were the finest young men in the whole world. I'd conveniently forget that Michigan and Notre Dame and Purdue recruited just as vigorously and got the same enthusiasm out of their programs. I can never remember a season when I didn't tell the whole world that our team had a chance to be a title contender. I guess in my heart I really believed that, and I'd have said the same thing if I had been coaching at Chickamauga Tech." Daugherty went on to muse that he once thought of tasking several freshman linemen with carrying him off the field each Saturday, whether in victory or defeat, for PR purposes. "Then the fans and the press would say, 'Look, there goes old Duffy again. He ain't much of a coach, but those players sure love him.'" The man who always had fun and made the best of every situation was probably correct in his self-analysis. Optimism was one of his virtues. He was consistently able to transfer both his passion and his confidence in the team to his players. Playing for Duffy was fun and positive. There was no reason for the coach to apologize for that.

There was nothing phony about Duffy's upbeat outlook or his love for people, according to Daugherty's daughter Dree. Hers is an interesting story, one that provides several insights into Hugh Daugherty. In February 1954, just after Daugherty had been named head coach at Michigan State, and while he and Francie were in Duffy's hometown of Barnesboro, the two received exciting news from the St. Vincent Home for Children. The baby they were going to adopt had been born. The Daughertys left Pennsylvania immediately for East Lansing to bring Dree Elizabeth Daugherty home. Dree told *Faith* magazine that her father's "perspective on life had great influence on me. Daddy was always optimistic and had a smile on his face. He always made the best of the situation. I approach my life this way as well. It is certainly more pleasant to approach challenges optimistically and happily." Dree also noted her father's warmth. Daugherty, born a Presbyterian, became a Roman Catholic in the early 1960s. "I remember waiting every Sunday before church," said Duffy's daughter fondly, remembering her days at St. Thomas Aquinas in East Lansing. "He had a hard time leaving anywhere—people always stopped and asked him for just one more thing. As a result, he would be late for church, which was embarrassing. As an adult, I am never late. But we always went as a family and never missed a week."

The Spartans opened the 1958 campaign by welcoming in a solid California team. The Spartans clicked in near midseason form as Daugherty used his starters sparingly in a 33-12 romp over the Golden Bears. It was an ideal win for Duffy, one that enabled the coach to get a good look at his overall roster as the Spartans rolled up 502 yards.

Next up was a spotty Michigan team. For the first time in during Daugherty's regime, the Wolverines would be coming to East Lansing. A celebrative throng of 76,434 crowded into the Spartan edifice anxious to watch their heroes take the measure of their arrogant intrastate neighbors. Michigan mentor Bennie Oosterbaan went to work on some special strategies for this contest. He had his team loop and stunt to confuse State, and one of his players really stepped up. End Gary Prahst stole a lateral and ran 41 yards for a score, then contributed to another TD by inducing a fumble with a jarring tackle. Michigan was off to a 12-0 lead. A State comeback was in order. Dean Look snared a punt and dashed 90 yards with the leather. A second TD followed, the result of a 97-yard drive. In the absence of successful PATs, however, the game ended in a 12-12 tie.

Eastern power Pitt visited a week later, the Spartans third consecutive home game. With Michigan State throwing just nine times for the game, the Spartans won handily 22-8. "We don't need more passing, just more completions," quipped Daugherty.

Despite a healthy 2-0-1 record, injuries were starting to accumulate, and Daugherty began making major personnel changes. The Spartans next packed their bags for West Lafayette, Indiana, and a date with troublesome Purdue. The Boilermakers had taken note of State's anemic aerial attack and dug in to stop the Spartan ground game. They did, holding State to just 38 rushing yards, and despite committing five fumbles themselves, the home team beat State for third time since 1953, 14-6.

With the offense sputtering, the Spartans went to Illinois, where the Illini pitched a 16-0 shutout. State had now scored just 18 points in its three conference games. A 3-1-1 Wisconsin team visited Michigan State the following week and also exposed the Spartans' offensive ineptitude in a 9-7 Badger win.

Now 2-3-1, and 0-3-1 in the conference, the deflated Green and White headed to Indiana to get well offensively against the always-hapless Hoosiers. This, however, was not a typical Indiana squad, and though only 18,000 fans showed up in Bloomington, the home team once again throttled the Spartan offense. The gamebreaker occurred when Hoosier star end Earl Faison, stuffed a State field goal attempt and sprinted 92 yards for the only score of the game in a 6-0 Hoosier victory.

The team was now 2-4-1 and looking for its first conference win. What was particularly maddening was that the problems were exclusively on the offensive side of the ball. In five conference games State had yielded just 57 points (11.4 a game), never more than 16. They had scored a puny 25.

After a series of highly successful seasons, the Spartans were not handling failure very well. In short, they had bottomed out, losing the following week to a hitherto winless Minnesota team. The Golden Gophers, losers of ten straight dating back to the 1957 campaign, walloped the visitors from East Lansing by an embarrassing 39-12 margin.

Perhaps worse than the losses was that all this was going on under the watchful eye of Biggie Munn, a Minnesota alum. Munn, having been rumored to be a candidate for the athletic director position at Minnesota, had brought a host of friends to Minneapolis for the game, fully expecting the Spartans to lay the lumber to the toothless Gophers. After the game Munn entered a Minneapolis restaurant, one of whose patrons was *Detroit News* sportswriter Pete Waldmeir. According to Waldmeir, an angry Munn headed over to his table and said, "I want to tell you fellows something. What happened out there today was terrible. I've never seen a poorer game." Then came the punch line. "It really hurts to see something you've built, an empire you have made with your own hands come tumbling down. It's tough. I tell you, really tough to watch things go to pieces like this."

There it was. Munn was taking credit for the entire run of success at State, his seven years at the helm in addition to the next four under Duffy. More important, he was pronouncing the period of success dead and fingering Daugherty as the culprit. Waldmeir telephoned his office and related the incident, believing it would be sidebar feature in the larger context of the game report. He was wrong. His editors ran Munn's comments on the first page of the news section.

The issue now was joined. It was time to choose sides when it came to Michigan State football. It was either Biggie or Duffy. The boat would not hold both. Both had their loyalists. Duffy's friends urged him to go directly to President Hannah and lay down the gauntlet: Make your choice—Biggie or me.

Daugherty said nothing. Hannah, however, had to do something. He called the two into his office and with the doors closed made his point in a most convincing fashion. Although only the three participants know what was said, all observers did see Duffy and Biggie leaving the office arm in arm. From that point on, a détente was in effect.

Superficial friendliness was expressed as each attended all appropriate university affairs. They did not mingle, however. Munn did not attend parties at the Daugherty home, and Duffy was not a guest at the socials in Munn's new five-bedroom residence.

Harking back to Munn's favorite saying, that the difference between good and great is just a little extra effort, writer Gerald Holland's summation of the Michigan State situation seemed apt. "In between these extremes of opinion stand a great many people who like and admire and get along with both Biggie Munn and Duffy Daugherty," he wrote in 1962. "They do not find it difficult. They find that all it takes (as Biggie says in his favorite maxim) is just a little extra effort."

The season came to a merciful close with a 26-7 win over a 3-6 Kansas State team in East Lansing. Michigan State, a team and a program fixed in the limelight for three glorious years, ended the season totally off the radar screen.

Going a ghastly 0-5-1 in the conference was particularly unsettling. Amazingly, State ranked 2nd in total yards on defense, first against the pass. The problems were on offense, where they Spartans scored the fewest points in league play and finished 9th in total offense, 8th in rushing.

No Spartan showed up in the rushing, passing, scoring, or total offense top ten. End Sam Williams did finish 7th in receiving yards, and Dean Look led the league in punt returning (32.5 yards per return) and was runner-up in punting at 40 yards per attempt. Williams and guard Ellison Kelly did manage to make the first-team All–Big Ten squad, with halfback Look named to the second.

The Munn-Daugherty era had made winning an expectation at State. Now there were questions about Duffy's coaching competence. Despite the sorry 1958 experience, some people most certainly did think Duffy could coach. After all, Daugherty still had gone 27-9-1 over the past four seasons, 30-15-1 when one adds on his inaugural 3-6 campaign. The Green Bay Packers, fresh from a 1-10-1 finish, needed a coach. They approached Duffy, and although Daugherty never took over Packer football fortunes, Green Bay did all right. They settled on Vince Lombardi.

But the losing and lack of respect hurt the genial leprechaun. A disgruntled alum sent the coach a less than complimentary letter. What was most upsetting to Daugherty were not the contents of the epistle but that it reached his desk addressed only to "Duffy the Dope."

CHAPTER 8

A Small Step Back

"Some kids have traveled more as seniors than the editors of *National Geographic*."

—Duffy on blue-chip recruits that visit many schools

A s the 1959 season approached, some reporters asked Duffy who he was most happy to see back for Michigan State. "Me," he replied.

Duffy needed players, and fortunately he knew how to recruit them. Most college coaches don't particularly enjoy talking about recruiting. It is not the most savory aspect of the business today, and it was even less so in previous eras. Fritz Howell, the great sportswriter of Duffy's era, once said he could remember a time when a triple-threat performer was an athlete who could run, kick and throw, rather than one being remunerated by the school, the alumni, and the downtown coaches. Duffy, however, spoke openly of recruiting and its import. "Our biggest job," he told *Time* magazine in a moment of both truth and overstatement, given the complexity of his coaching system, "is recruiting. The thing we do least is coach. Eighty percent of winning football is material. More football games are won from December to September when most recruiting is done than from September to December."

"Once in a while an underdog will become inspired and upset a favorite," he told Holland of *Sports Illustrated*. "But most of the time the team that wins will be the team with the most good football players. That's why we go out and recruit the best high school football players we can find. That's the real art of winning football games. There are no geniuses out there."

Daugherty did not like the "letter of intent" a youngster is enjoined to sign once he has decided on a college. "A boy should have the right to make up his mind without pressure from anybody," the coach told Edgar Hayes, the editor of the *Detroit Times*, in a conversation in 1956. According to Daugherty the method of recruiting should be low key. "We don't try to *sell* a boy. If he likes the school and needs help, then we sit down with him and try to figure things out." Duffy's easy air was not lost on his coaching staff. "I'll tell you something," said one of his assistants, "before a game I get sick to my stomach. And Duffy? He can take a nap." There were things that did get to him, however. "He's not perfect," the assistant added. "He's the world's worst loser at gin rummy."

To the extent that Daugherty's description of his method is at all accurate, it may be an indicator of why he was successful. Beyond the charm of his personality, Daugherty had the knack for putting people at ease and keeping them comfortable, while at the same time not wanting to lose. Add that to the beauty of the Red Cedar River campus, a winning football team, and rabid fan base, and the cumulative pull could be irresistible.

Again, before his time, Duffy Daugherty knew the intricacies of successful recruiting. He was careful to give tender loving attention to the two sources of so much of his talent, the high school coaches and the proud parents of the high school stars. "Duffy is the finest football banquet speaker I've ever heard," testified a president of the Michigan High School Coaches Association. "He gets right down where they [the audience] live. He appeals to mom and dad." No one went untouched in Daugherty's method of what in today's business vernacular might be called circular marketing. He stayed close to the coaches and doted about kids in front of their parents and alums in need of tickets or some information. Always accessible, Duffy made time to banter with old friends, hear out a coach about a would-be Spartan, and comfort a mother worried about her gone-to-college son.

Moreover, the coach knew the pluses of Michigan State, and despite his claims to the contrary, sold them without reservation in his own unique way. He touted the winning football tradition built by Biggie Munn and John Hannah and the football frenzy extant among the students and the Lansing community. He promoted the pastoral beauty of the campus on the banks of the Red Cedar River, as well as the topflight athletic and recreational facilities the university provided. In short, there was much to sell, and Daugherty never tired of selling it.

In 1959, there was a substantial problem, and Daugherty turned his team in to the infractions committee because he found one of his assistants had been paying some of the players. He then alerted the Big Ten commissioner, Bill Reed, and told him it had been corrected. At one point every team in the conference was cheating, due to the "need factor" policy.

The need factor method involved determining a given athlete's ability to pay for his own education and subtracting that from the cost. The need gap was picked up by the university. This Big Ten rule was wreaking havoc with its members' ability to compete with schools from rival conferences that granted full scholarships. Cheating was rife as each school played fast and loose with its need computations. In any case, Commissioner Reed finally got an agreement from the coaches to offer no more than room, board, tuition, and books, in exchange for the end of the need factor.

In Daugherty's early years, his principal competitors were Michigan and Notre Dame, estimable foes indeed. As college football became more and more big-time, and recruiting evolved into a national enterprise, players became the objects of bidding in an environment with minimal NCAA vigilance. Fathers would pit one school's offer against another, opening the gates to gross corruption.

Daugherty's suspicions about illegal recruiting were aroused whenever he thought he had a recruit committed to MSU only to have to go back repeatedly to resell the youngster who had now visited any number of rival schools. One thing he did not sell was education, realizing a first-rate education was obtainable many schools. One edge he had, however, was that Duffy could assure almost any blue-chipper he would play early at State, whereas the same youngster might find himself stockpiled at Notre Dame or Alabama. And Duffy had his own little bag of recruiting tools. "I had two recruiting pitches," he said. If he talked with a native of the state, Duffy hit hard on "state pride." If the lad was from out of state, the focus was on how it was those who tore up roots and put down new ones that made our nation great.

Families, particularly mothers, were the key. A story often told about two-time Heisman Trophy winner Archie Griffin alleges that on Thanksgiving Day, Northwestern's Johnny Pont, who felt he had an inside shot at Griffin, debated as to whether he should call the Griffin family on a holiday. After painful deliberation, he opted to make the call, only to find out that Woody Hayes was in the kitchen carving the turkey. Daugherty loved the yarn about the divorced coach who courted more than the athlete in question on his recruiting trips. After a number of romantic interludes with the player's mother, the woman told the anxious coach that, although her son had decided to go to Houston, she would be coming to his school to work on her graduate degree.

Duffy enjoyed telling the self-deprecating story about his efforts to recruit a young man named Tom Schoen. Duffy was speaking at a banquet in Cleveland, ready to trot out one of his favorite stories. Luxuriating in the attention he was receiving, Daugherty decided to make certain he brought down the house by imitating the speech impediment of the farmer in the story. Duffy left the howling and eagerly sought an introduction to Tom Schoen's father. Of course, Mr. Schoen had a speech impediment similar to that of the butt of Duffy's story.

"Naturally, I thought he was putting me on," Duffy said. "He even told me he enjoyed the story, so I continued my conversation with him, all the time pretending to have the impediment. It seemed real funny at the time, except that Mr. Schoen really did talk like the farmer."

Tom Schoen went to Notre Dame.

A major Michigan State asset was the commitment of President John Hannah to the football program. Hannah, realizing the critical nature of recruiting, was eager to help. He met families, engaging in bonding talk regarding a youth's academic background, religious affiliation, and hobbies. He was needed because Michigan was only too happy to denigrate its in-state rival as a "cow college."

As for talent, "Good athletes just stick out just like that," noted Daugherty. They have a presence, a natural mien that the more ordinary athlete does not possess. And they make a difference. "If you have a great team, you'll have maybe six or seven super athletes on your sixty-man roster," he explained. "You'll have about 35 to 40 average athletes. But the six or seven with exceptional skills are the ones who'll make the difference in your season." They are also under unique pressure, because they are the ones expected to make plays, as former college and NFL coach Jimmy Johnson would say.

Dean Look may well have been Duffy's favorite player because of his willingness to do whatever the team needed in 1959, what was for Daugherty a pivotal year. Prior to his senior year, Daugherty asked Look to consider moving from halfback to a position he had never played, quarterback. Turning down a $50,000 baseball bonus in the process, the young man became an All-American.

In contrast to previous years, Michigan State received no significant preseason mention, not even in the Big Ten. The conventional thinking was that with twenty-four lettermen returning and Daugherty's job in peril, the Spartans would be stronger. Nonetheless, things did not look all that promising. The team had only two established linemen, Captain Don Wright, a guard who had been shifted from center, and Palmer Pyle, a tackle. The backfield appeared sound with the multithreat Dean Look now at quarterback, Blanche Martin back from knee surgery, and a sophomore with good running skills named Gary Ballman. And Duffy was tinkering with his impotent offense, employing a new formation, a double-wing T. That, and greater speed, made State at best a dark horse in the Big Ten.

A weak Texas A&M team came to East Lansing to open the season. That only 49,507 fans showed up is an indicator of the limited optimism for 1959 among State rooters. The Green and White did nothing to drive expectations upward as they fell 9-7 in an upset engineered by A&M quarterback Charlie Milstead.

Once again, offense was the problem. The game marked the fifth time in the last ten outings that the Spartans had failed to hit double figures, the seventh time that they failed to score more than a dozen points in a game.

A crowd of 103,234 waited for the Spartans to enter Michigan Stadium the following week. The Ann Arbor air agreed with Duffy's troops, as they laid a 34-8 spanking on the Wolverines. It appeared the scoring drought had been broken. It had, but only for one week. Iowa's quarterback Olen Treadway had his best passing day (two TDs) as the Hawkeyes ripped MSU 37-8 in Iowa City.

Notre Dame was back on the schedule after a year's respite. The Irish always drew a huge crowd, and despite State's lackluster 1-2 mark, 73,480 fans were on hand for renewal of hostilities. The Spartan defense rushed quarterback George Izo ferociously and stopped one Irish drive just a yard from the goal line. Meanwhile, Dean Look was all the rage. He set up one touchdown with 41-yard jaunt, and passed 52 yards for another as the Green and White posted a rousing 19-0 win.

Indiana (3-1) was aiming at its second straight winning season when State headed for Bloomington on October 24. In a defensive confrontation, State barely hung on, 14-6, as center Larry Cundiff proved a stalwart as the Spartans denied the Hoosiers on four line smashes late in the game. There was good news and bad news awaiting the Spartans the following week. The bad news was that the opponent was Ohio State. The good news was that the Buckeyes were just 2-3 and would be coming into East Lansing. The bad news won out, as Tom Matte threw for three scores in a 30-24 win, driving the MSU record down to .500.

The unpredictable Spartans came right back the next week and beat Purdue 15-0 at home, as Look fired two touchdown passes, one of 28 yards to Gary Ballman and the other for 48 yards to Jim Corgiat. Then, when the Purdue line proved too stubborn for the State offense, Art Brandstatter kicked a 23-yard field goal. The Spartans followed that victory with a surprising 15-10 win over a 6-1 Northwestern team, on the strength of stacked defenses designed to stop the elusive Ron Burton. Look again was the offensive star, hitting seven of seven passes and going over the goal line for the winning TD.

Amazingly, although the Spartans were just 5-3 for the season, they were very much in the running for the league championship. In a season of parity, their 4-2 record was identical to that of Wisconsin and Northwestern, and a nose ahead of Illinois and Purdue's 3-2-1 mark. There was a hitch, however. The Big Ten season was over for the Spartans—their final game was a night contest in Miami—while the other two co-leaders still had a conference game left to play.

Daugherty kept his eye on the afternoon's Big Ten activity with great interest. Illinois took care of a skidding Northwestern team with authority, routing the Wildcats 28-0 in Champaign. Wisconsin was pitted against Minnesota in a nationally televised game, with one of the viewers most certainly being Duffy Daugherty. In the third quarter, Minnesota held a 7-0 lead and was down on the Wisconsin ten. Sandy Stephens, the Gophers' ace quarterback, then floated a pass out in the flat, only to have it picked by a Badger and returned for a touchdown. Bad as it was, a tie would still send the Spartans to Pasadena. It wasn't to be. In the fourth quarter, Stephens was intercepted again. The Badgers mustered a field goal and their tickets for Pasadena were punched.

The season had a bitter end. State was sufficiently demoralized to fall 18-13 in the south Florida rain that evening, as the Gators' 152-pound quarterback Fran Curci set up one TD and scored another.

Michigan State finished the season 5-4. It was a small step back from the 1958 disappointment.

Despite contending, they were not at all a powerful team, outscoring their Big Ten opponents by barely 3 points a game. Moreover, they were a team of extremes, ranking #2 in total offense, eighth in defense. All-American Dean Look, who finished #2 in passing and #3 in total offense, was State's lone representative on the All–Big Ten first (or second) team.

Despite two consecutive less than stellar campaigns, Duffy Daugherty had made his mark in the world of college football coaching, and the phone was ringing. USC, impressed with his achievements in the shadow of the mighty University of Michigan, offered him the head coaching position. Duffy, with the president of Michigan State very much in his corner, coupled with an ever-optimistic outlook toward the Spartans' football future, decided Green and White were still his favorite colors.

CHAPTER 9

Ups and Downs

"Let's face it, anyone can carry a football. The thing only weighs thirteen ounces."

—Former lineman Duffy Daugherty

The times were changing in 1960 and the Big Ten coaches did not like it. More specifically, they were again unhappy with the strict academic controls placed on aid to players. In short, the system mandated that a lad's parents pay as much of the college bill as they could, with the school making up the rest. So much for full athletic scholarships. It was suggested that Missouri and Kansas benefited more from the limitations of the Big Ten aid plan than any other schools in the country. And it didn't end with fewer dollars. The plan required higher academic standards for incoming athletes. According to the commissioner's office, "More than three-fourths of the Big Ten students receiving grant-in-aid support last year ranked in the upper quarter of their high school classes."

The Big Ten was bowing to national pressure put on intercollegiate athletics "to bring football back to its rightful place" within the academic community. In 1956 *Sports Illustrated* did a study of the Big Ten, likely the most prestigious football conference in the nation. The magazine cited a marked increase in athletic recruitment, a sharp upward spike in the amount and often dubious nature of financial aid to athletes, the practice of extending academic favors to athletes, and violations of recruiting rules.

The league commissioned its own study in that year and decided to tighten things up. In its report, the league committee predicted in Orwellian tones what would become of the future of big-time college athletics if the current system was not overhauled: "All students engaged in intercollegiate athletics will be carefully screened, selected and vigorously recruited . . . on the basis of terms arrived at in bargaining between the coach and prospect or his agent. . . . Complete financial assistance will be provided, (exceeding) mere educational expense and sufficient to maintain a high standard of living. . . . Discontinuance of non-revenue producing intercollegiate sports and intra-mural activities. . . . A state of disunity amounting to virtual anarchy . . . in the administration of rules and regulations. . . . Athletes segregated in all campus activities from student bodies at large. . . . The Big Ten . . . will emerge as a closed corporation displaying the ultimate in athletic prowess at any level. . . . In fact, it may well form a functional arrangement in the nature of a farm system, with organized professional sports.

"At a certain point, either educational administrators will recognize there is no identity between their sports and educational programs and will order the dissolution of the former before the attachment corrupts the latter; or the distinction between intercollegiate sports and professional sports will become so invisible that public support will shift to the latter . . . and the resulting financial chaos will force abandonment of the intercollegiate program."

On another front, free substitution was slowly leaking back into college football, as the substitution rule permitted the platooning of teams. Although a positive step on the surface, one could argue that this worked against the Big Ten because now, more than ever, schools needed to have many more quality football players to be competitive.

Problematic though all this was, for Duffy the issue was winning. He yearned to return to the top of the national football polls after a combined 8-9-1 record over the past two seasons. There was some guarded Rose Bowl talk in East Lansing as the 1960 seasoned dawned. The Big Ten conference figured to be down a bit, opening the gate to a run for the roses by a fair-to-middling Spartan team. The running game looked forceful with Herb Adderley and Gary Ballman. Moreover, the defensive line was formidable, although the offensive interior appeared slow and inexperienced, anchored by center Dave Manders. Daugherty had done his recruiting, however, as there would be lots of sophomore talent—the best in the conference—vying for playing time.

The Spartan season opened against a Mike Ditka–led Pittsburgh team in Duffy's home state of Pennsylvania. Donning earphones and dispatching messengers to the huddle with plays, Duffy watched State escape with a miraculous 7-7 tie. With just two minutes left in the first half, Pitt broke a scoreless deadlock on a Dave Kraus to Mike Ditka strike. The Michigan State offense continued to perform lifelessly in the second half. Down 7-0 with only five seconds left, quarterback Tom Wilson lofted one deep in the direction of Jason Harness. The ball deflected off defender Ed Sharockman and caromed into Harness's arms for a 66-yard touchdown.

Michigan then came to Red Cedar River country and struck first with a 99-yard kickoff return by Denny Fitzgerald. Daugherty, taking advantage of the more liberal substitution rules, shuttled players in and out, wearing down the Wolverines. When fullback Carl Charon led a late charge and went over for a touchdown, the Spartans had a 24-17 win.

Now 1-0-1, Duffy prepared his team for the powerful Iowa Hawkeyes and their quick backs. The Hawkeyes were much improved over 1959, when they finished 5-4. This was the one to get. With but three minutes left in the fourth quarter, and leading 15-14, the Spartans were on the march, down at the Iowa thirty-one. On a third and two in an era in which a couple of runs almost certainly would have garnered a first down, lightning struck in the form of Joe Williams. The ball popped out of the arms of the State ball carrier, only to be picked off in midair by the Iowa sophomore and returned 67 yards for a score. A last-minute Hawkeye interception swelled the margin to a 27-15 final count.

State bounced back a week later against a weak (2-8 for the season) Notre Dame team, 21-0, in South Bend. Another Indiana foe was next, and the result was the same. The Green and White smoked the Hoosiers 35-0 in Bloomington in what was deemed a nonconference game because Indiana had been ruled ineligible in the league that year. Big linemen were being noticed around college football and one of the best was State's Dave Behrman, who had trimmed down to 247 pounds after weighing 285. "He looks like a starved giant," remarked Duffy. "I knew he could be our finest defensive lineman, and he hasn't let us down."

Woody Hayes brought his mighty 4-1 Buckeyes into East Lansing a week later. With only one conference loss, the Spartans were still very much alive in the league race. Hayes hammered the Michigan State line all day with fullback Bob Ferguson and quarterback Tom Matte, such that the MSU defense was not ready when Woody turned halfback Bob Klein loose. He ran virtually unnoticed for a 46-yard TD in a 21-10 Buckeye win.

Duffy now really needed a win to avoid having the now 3-2-1 Spartans fall back to .500. A 2-3-1 but always problematic Purdue team, one that had already beaten Ohio State, was waiting for the Spartans in West Lafayette, Indiana.

Purdue's Roy Walker, a third-string fullback who had never carried the ball in a Big Ten game, took over for injured Willie Jones in the first quarter and scored two touchdowns. Duffy, however, had a third-string fullback of his own, George Saimes, who spearheaded a 99-yard fourth-quarter drive culminated by a 1-yard plunge by quarterback Tom Wilson. State won 17-13.

The 4-2-1 Spartans had only one Big Ten date left, at Northwestern against the 4-3 Ara Parseghian–coached Wildcats. Daugherty did some savvy maneuvering, shifting interior assignments to improve gap blocking, and State pulled off three trap plays for long TDs—two by fullback Ron Hatcher (51 and 32 yards) and one 74-yarder by Gary Ballman. Art Brandstatter hit three PATs, and the Spartans escaped Evanston, Illinois, with a 21-18 win.

The Spartans ran their record to a highly respectable 6-2-1, beating the University of Detroit 43-15 to end the season.

It was a crazy conference season, with Wisconsin playing seven league games and Michigan State but five, owing to the Indiana matter. While the 3-2 Spartans solved their offensive problems (they were one of just three Big Ten teams to average 300 yards a game) they struggled on defense, yielding 315 yards per game. They were outscored by just under 2 points a contest, much due to their permitting 19.2 points per game, and yielded a turnover a game more than their opposition. Halfback Herb Adderley was the team's star, mainly on defense. He and end Fred Arbanas made the league's first and second all-conference teams, respectively.

Football is an emotional game, and 1961 was an emotional season.

Duffy Daugherty, bent on turning the Spartans into a power, put the team in chains, literally. During the summer workouts, the coach had the players wear weighted bracelets around their ankles and wrists. A conditioning adherent, Daugherty would toughen the Green and White. Michigan State was now a veteran team—twenty-six lettermen back—such that talented end Matt Snorton and linebacker Charley Migyanka figured to be the only sophomores to crack the starting platoons. Gary Ballman, Ron

Hatcher, and Carl Charon gave the squad a solid backfield, behind end Art Brandstatter, tackle Jim Bobbitt, and guard Ed Budde. It was the year, however, of the accidental quarterback, Pete Smith was a walk-on, and as Duffy put it, "More often than not, a walk-on walks out unnoticed three or four days after walking on." Pete's case, however, was different. State had recruited two quarterbacks the year previous, but both were baseball stars as well and left to seek their fortunes on the diamonds of major league baseball. Smith, all of 165 pounds, might, according to Daugherty, be mistaken as a busboy at a team banquet. Smith was the team's question mark.

Despite some difficult seasons, there was no confusion in Daugherty as to what it took to win. In *Defense Spartan Style* he noted the importance of (1) having the personnel, (2) being fundamentally sound as a coach, (3) communicating one's knowledge effectively, (4) being sufficiently flexible to cope with changing formations, and (5) being capable of confusing an offense with different looks. Were one to substitute a few words here and there to make his views applicable to both sides of the ball, one would have the essence of Duffy Daugherty's theory of successful coaching.

The Spartans were slated to start the season in Madison, Wisconsin, against the Badgers. Duffy sagely conceded the short passing game to Wisconsin's Ron Miller, who went 16-25 and 184 yards, while denying everything else. With the junior native of Ecorse, Michigan, Pete Smith at the controls, the Spartans rolled over a strong (6-3 for the season) Badger team, 20-0 in Camp Randall. The following week, Stanford visited East Lansing and was treated rudely by the Spartans to the tune of 31-3.

Smith's father was at the game. Amid the excitement, the proud father died in the stands. With the funeral scheduled for Thursday of that week, Smith was gone, leaving a stunned team hardly speaking as they mechanically ground through their practices in preparation for a date with Michigan at the Big House the following Saturday. Smith said he would be back for practice on Thursday, so Daugherty postponed drills for a half an hour. The team had been out on the field for quite a while when suddenly Smith appeared. The backup quarterback, without being prompted, trotted off to make way for Smith.

The players were quiet when Pete entered the huddle. He looked at them and said simply, "I didn't come back here to lose to Michigan." With Michigan rooters occasionally howling "moo" at the Spartans, the two teams did battle in a rivalry that began in 1898 when the Wolverines stooped to play the agricultural school. Michigan won that game 39-0, and four years later smashed their humble intrastate rivals 119-0. State did not win until 1913 (12-7), but until 1950 Michigan owned the series, going

33-6. Duffy, however, had his way with the Wolverines, posting a 4-2-1 record over his first seven seasons.

A war of poor-mouthing preceded this one. "We have 12 good football players," said Michigan mentor Bump Elliott, "Michigan State has 24."

"That's nonsense," Duffy rejoined, realizing the Wolverines had destroyed their first two foes by a combined 67-14. "They used 58 players in their first two games. The way they talk, if we win it's because we have better players, but if they win it's because they are better coached."

State got the early jump in this one, recovering a Wolverine bobble at the 31 on the second play from scrimmage. Led by 6'4" 213-pound Herman Johnson, the Spartans plowed the 31 yards to a 7-0 advantage. The Green and White made it 14-0 by scoring on a 76-yard drive the second time they got the ball, with the key play a 46-yard Smith to Matt Snorton aerial strike. Michigan had a second-quarter touchdown called back and came up short on four line smashes inside the State 5 in the third quarter. That was it as the Spartans romped to 28-0 win, with one of the scores a Smith-to-Charon TD through the air.

The Smith tragedy was not the only one of its type for Daugherty and his Spartans. In the late 1960s the father of Ron and Rich Saul died the night before a game. After the news was broken to the twins, the two talked with their mother and decided to play the game against Wisconsin the following day, a victory in which they played with tremendous intensity, before leaving to join the family.

Now considered the best in the Midwest, State next played host to Notre Dame. For thirty uncomfortable minutes, 76,132 fans watched the Irish push State around, gaining 170 yards while holding MSU to but 12 yards on the ground posting a 7-0 halftime lead.

Daugherty went to work at the break. He altered all the offensive blocking assignments and showed the defensive backs how they were to rotate to meet the plays. He employed tackles Jim Bobbitt and Dave Behrman, along with guard Ed Budde, together on both sides of the ball. He also moved defensive back George Saimes to offense. With the line blowing open holes, Saimes ran for two TDs (24 and 25 yards), and Art Brandstatter added a field goal to make the score 17-7.

The Spartans then pounded Indiana 35-0 a week later, setting up a confrontation of two monstrous lines, as the Spartans, #1 in the country, headed for Minneapolis to play the 4-1 Minnesota Golden Gophers.

Master of the psychological though he was, Duffy had no answer for the team's funk when they visited the land of Paul Bunyan. Minnesota had barely won the Little Brown Jug 23-20 at home against Michigan, a team State had demolished by four touchdowns. Sandy Stephens was the star. In addition to throwing for a touchdown, Stephens sealed the Gophers' 13-0 win by intercepting a Spartan pass in the end zone in the final minute. "I know we weren't ready for the game," mourned the coach who once again saw an undefeated season slip away on a flat effort, "and it's such a helpless feeling."

The Gophers defeated a Spartan squad that had yielded only 10 points in its first five games—contests including Wisconsin, Michigan, and Notre Dame. The 13 Minnesota points, however, still should not have beaten the Green and White. State mounted three monstrous drives deep into Gopher territory, only to come up short in the red zone each time.

The worst was yet to come. Perhaps the toughest game the Spartans played in the up-and-down 1961 year was the one against Purdue and its battering offensive style, in West Lafayette. Needing a tie against the 4-2 Boilermakers to keep their Rose Bowl hopes alive, the Spartans went down to a 7-6 defeat on a stuffed extra point.

Sophomore Sherman Lewis perked up the offense with two TD runs in a 21-13 win over Northwestern a week later, but the Spartans were now out of the Big Ten hunt, having been eliminated by Minnesota and Ohio State the week before. A 34-7 blowout of winless Illinois gave the Spartans a 7-2 season.

The Spartans finished with the league's top defense, yielding 201 yards per game, only 90 of which were on the ground. Their 313.7 offensive yards per game were second only to Ohio State. Individually, Sherman Lewis and George Saimes ranked 3rd and 8th respectively in rushing, with Smith ranking 5th in passing. Saimes and Behrman made the All–Big Ten first team, Lewis the second.

The season ended emotionally for the forty-six-year-old coach. Despite going 7-2, Duffy was hanged in effigy after the season-ending rout of Illinois in East Lansing.

Hugh "Duffy" Daugherty.

A youthful Duffy
Daugherty, embarking
on a storied coaching
future.

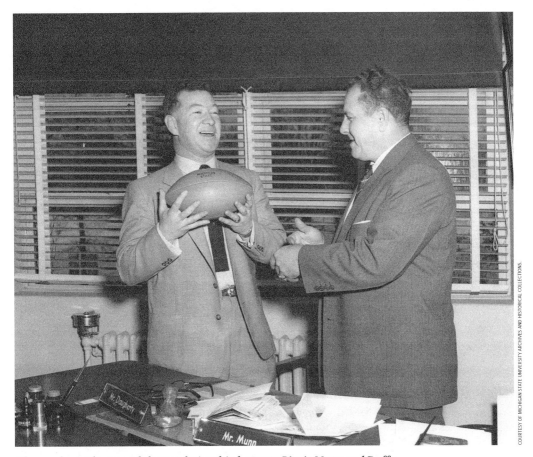

A happy day in the up-and-down relationship between Biggie Munn and Duffy.

Clarence L. "Biggie" Munn, Duffy's predecessor as head coach (1947–53) and Daugherty's athletic director (1954–71). Munn was sixty-six when he died in 1975.

Duffy (*kneeling left*) and Biggie Munn (*center*) in Duffy's days as an assistant on Munn's staff. During his tenure as head coach, Munn set a high bar for Duffy, going 54-9-2 as head coach. His 1952 squad finished the season undefeated (9-0-0) and ranked #1 in the country. Note "MSC" for Michigan State College, before the institution reached university status in 1955.

The Spartans, with Head Coach Biggie Munn and Assistant Duffy Daugherty, celebrating their 28-20 win over UCLA in the 1954 Rose Bowl.

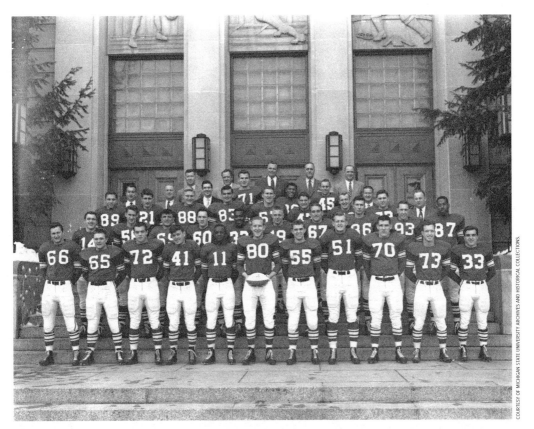

Michigan State Spartans, 1953 Big Ten Champions and winners of the 1954 Rose Bowl. It was Biggie's final season before turning the program over to Duffy.

John A. Hannah, Michigan State president from 1941 to 1969. Hannah was a strong advocate for integration.

1965 Michigan State Spartans.

The great Charles "Bubba" Smith, #95, ready to wreak havoc on an opponent. The two-time all-American in 1965 and 1966 died in 2011.

Steve Juday, All-American Spartan QB, was co-captain and MVP of the 1965 team.

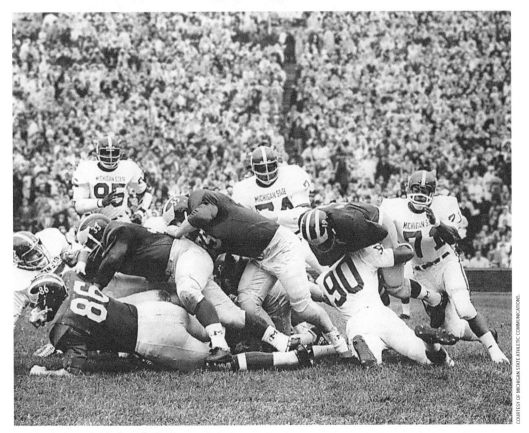

All-American (1965 and 1966) George Webster, #90, stopping a Wolverine cold.

November 19, 1966, "Kissing Your Sister."

Jimmy Raye, Fayetteville, North Carolina, a
member of Duffy's "Underground Railroad"
from the South. He was one of early African
American quarterbacks in college football,
leading the Spartans to a 9-0-1 mark in 1966.
Raye had huge shoes to fill. His predecessor,
Steve Juday, was captain of the 1965
championship team.

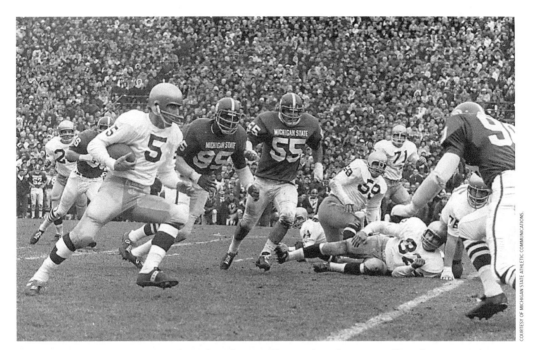

Notre Dame's Terry Hanratty, in the sights of #95 Bubba Smith and #55 Pat Gallinagh.

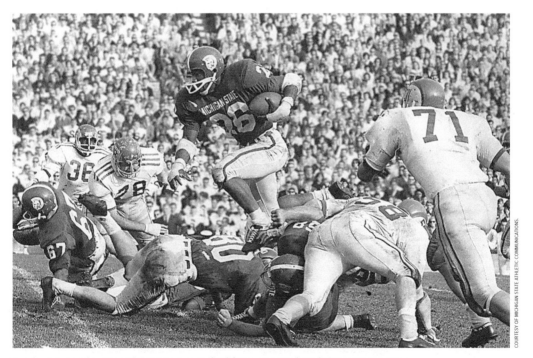

Leading ground gainer Clinton Jones rushed for 2,034 yards in his Spartan career.

Jimmy Raye, ready to launch.

Duffy, with 1966 All-Americans. (*Left to right*) running back Clinton Jones, kicker Dick Kenney, defensive end Bubba Smith, pass receiver Gene Washington, and roverback George Webster.

1966 Michigan State Spartans.

Spartan RB Clinton Jones. He was inducted into College Football Hall of Fame in 2015.

Gene Washington, an All-American in 1965 and 1966, and inducted into the College Football Hall of Fame in 2012.

End Gene Washington caught 106 passes for 1,938 yards over three seasons (1964–66).

QB Jimmy Raye was an even greater threat on the ground than in the air. Raye went on to a distinguished coaching career in college and the NFL.

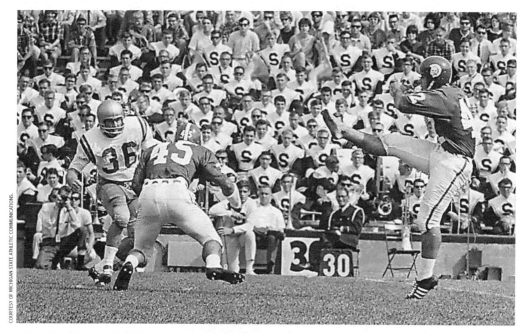

A barefoot blast by Dick Kenney. He and RB Bobby Apisa hailed from Hawaii.

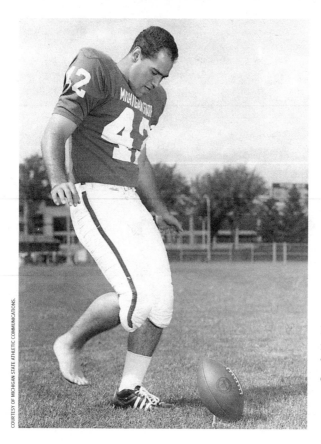

Kicker Dick Kenney was nationally known as the "barefoot kicker." Kenney died in 2005.

George Webster, from Anderson, South Carolina, another member of Duffy's "underground railroad." An All-American in 1965 and 1966, he died in 2007.

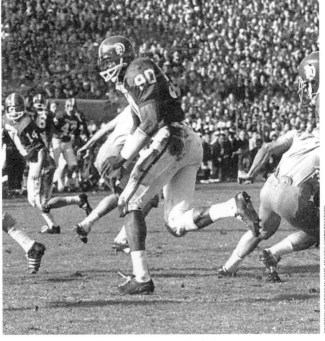

Roverback George Webster, a member of the College Football Hall of Fame, was named athletic director of Gulf Coast Community Services in Houston, working every day with underprivileged children.

Now silver-haired, Duffy, prowling the sidelines late in the season on a cold football day. Note the snow against the stands.

The Duffy Daugherty Football Building, a state-of-the-art memorial to Duffy's legacy at Michigan State.

Duffy Daugherty and family.

CHAPTER 10

Settled In

"Three things can happen when you put a football in the air, and two of them are bad."

T he 1962 season was filled with promise. After the 1958 debacle (3-5-1 overall and 0-5-1 in the Big Ten) Duffy had righted the ship. His Spartans had improved their record each of the three years since 1958 (5-4, 6-2-1, and 7-2) and figured to do even better in 1962. His backfield contained over 1,200 returning rushing yards in the form of George Saimes, Sherman Lewis, and Dewey Lincoln. There is an old saw that goes, if you have two quarterbacks, you have no quarterback. Duffy, however, had four candidates from which to choose. He also had stellar linemen Behrman, Snorton, Bobbitt, Budde, and (end) Ernie Clark back. Moreover, the schedule seemed to be have a Green and White smile as well. The Spartans would meet Michigan, Minnesota, and Purdue in East Lansing, and Ohio State not at all.

A trip to California—always a recruiting lure—started the season for State. Daugherty would match his squad against Stanford, coached by his friend, Jack Curtice. Although the Spartans hung the first score on the board, making it 7-0, Stanford's huge interior line was shutting down the State inside ground game. When Duffy pushed to the outside, Stanford adjusted by widening its six-man line, aiding its linebackers in flattening the speedy Spartan runners. On offense, Stanford quarterback Steve Thurlow attacked the MSU secondary effectively. Stan Lindskog hit on a 24-yard field goal, and sophomore John Payes ripped down the sidelines for a 33-yard TD to give the home team a 16-13 upset win. Curtice, a quipster like Duffy, seemed serious when he said, "We outhustled them."

The huge Spartans took out their frustrations on North Carolina the following week, 38-6. Next came Michigan. A rabid throng of 77,501 showed up for the team's confrontation with its neighbors from Ann Arbor. A Michigan assistant coach said, "I wish they'd cut out that moo stuff. You can see the hair stand up on the necks of those State kids. They want to kill us." In this one, however, there was little in the way of "Cow College" and "Moo" jeers heard as State dissolved all of the bitter taste of its season-opening loss by pulverizing the Wolverines 28-0.

The rivalry was intense, at least on the banks of the Red Cedar River. "One game doesn't make a season," said Daugherty in overstatement, "but this one has grown so big it pales the Army-Navy game in interest." When State registered a 14-7 win in 1950, after years of gridiron servitude to Michigan, East Lansing came apart. Rioting students hollered, partied, and turned over cars, resulting in myriad arrests. Though more civilized, there was much hooting after this rout in which 154-pound Sherman Lewis raced for three touchdowns as State picked up 391 yards rushing to Michigan's 72. Although Michigan still held at 35-16-4 series edge, Duffy was now 6-2-1 against the Wolverines.

The Spartans were a happy 3-1 a week later, when with the Notre Dame fans yelling, "Joe must go," in South Bend, George Saimes ran for 54, 49, and 15 yard TDs as MSU downed Joe Kuharich's Irish 31-7. Saimes blasted loose for another three scores in a 26-8 win over Indiana a week later.

Always troublesome Minnesota was next. The 3-1-1 Gophers, sporting the nation's best defense, had registered four shutouts in its first five games before heading for East Lansing. The Spartans, however, were the best ground team in the country. The winner of this one could well have the inside track to the championship and a trip to Pasadena, although Northwestern and Wisconsin were also still in the hunt. Something had to give, and it was State, as tackles Bobby Bell and Carl Eller held MSU to 30 yards rushing in a surprisingly one-sided 28-7 win. The Minnesota experience lingered. State bumbled away a 17-9 game to Purdue a week later in East Lansing.

Suddenly a middling 4-3, Duffy took his squad to Evanston, Illinois, to face the

6-1 Northwestern Wildcats, fresh from a loss to Wisconsin, now also 6-1. The latter two teams, along with Minnesota and Purdue, each had only one conference defeat.

The ever-resourceful Daugherty used an NFL-like four-man front to counter the Northwestern pro-type offense. He employed three blitzing linebackers behind massive tackles Behrman and Budde. Quarterback Tom Myers was harried all day, and the State defense flattened would-be draw plays. With Saimes and Lewis lugging the ball, State hammered the Wildcats 31-7, despite four costly fumbles.

With Purdue losing to Minnesota, the Gophers would face the Badgers in a winner-take-all game for the title the following week in Madison. While the Badgers polished off the Gophers 14-6, the Spartans were aiming at finishing the campaign 6-3 against the hapless (1-7) Illini in Champaign. At the end of a grueling day, Michigan State was 5-4 and Illinois 2-7, as the Illini made a second-quarter TD stand up in a 7-6 win.

It was a schizoid season offensively, as the team averaged 30.8 points per game in its five wins, and less than 9 (8.8) in the quartet of defeats. Defense was the backbone of the 1962 Spartans. Only one team, Minnesota, scored more than 17 points against the State defense, and only three reached double figures.

The middling State squad—3-3 in the Big Ten—was in the middle of the conference pack in scoring and scoring defense despite outscoring their opposition by a touchdown a game (17.8-11.2). This was largely due to their walloping Michigan, Indiana, and Northwestern by an 85-15 margin. The real strength of the Spartans was defense, finishing on top of the heap in total defensive yardage (179.3 per game). They allowed the fewest passing yards (68.5 per game, with no one else permitting less than 100) and second fewest yards on the ground (110.8). Turnovers proved the team's downfall, with the Green and White at –3 per game.

State had the league's #2 rushing attack, led by George Saimes, Dewey Lincoln, and Sherman Lewis, who finished 2nd, 4th, and 6th, respectively. The trio combined for just under 200 yards per game (193.8). Lewis was runner-up in scoring, with 40 points, while Herman Johnson won the interception title, snaring four enemy aerials. Center Dave Behrman and George Saimes were named to the All–Big Ten first team; end Matt Snorton and Lewis were on the second unit. Fullback Saimes was a consensus All-American pick as well.

Daugherty offered some typical Duffytalk as 1963 loomed. "We'll go into this season with maybe 6 to 8 men of demonstrated Big Ten quality," he said. "Almost all of our regular linemen will be gone. We'll have to settle on a quarterback, build passing and kicking games, and find power runners to spell our little backs. Our defensive backfield is a big, nebulous uncertainty." Other than that, all was well in East Lansing with Lewis and Lincoln returning in addition to halfback Ron Rubick and fullback Ron Lopes. Dick Proebstle and Charlie Migyanka would do battle for the quarterback post.

There was joy in East Lansing as MSU rolled over North Carolina 31-0 in the opener, with soccer-style kicker Lou Bobich hitting one from twenty-five and barely missing another from forty-three yards out. Amid the glee, however, there was concern that for the second straight year the team did not have a solid quarterback.

A trip to Los Angeles to meet powerful USC was next. Sophomore quarterback Steve Juday flipped a screen pass to Lewis, who took it for an 88-yard TD. Bobich then hit on a 38-yard three-pointer and it was 10-0. And that was it for the Spartans on offense. In the fourth quarter USC halfback Mike Garrett broke loose for a 52-yard touchdown jaunt on a trap. Then, only a few minutes later, on a 4th and 8, Hal Bedsole made a shoestring grab of a Pete Beathard pass in the end zone and State was hung with a 13-10 loss.

Down as the coach was as he trudged off the field, a moment of great elevation, one that would mark 1963 as a watershed year in his career, awaited him. After the game, Dr. Hannah summoned Daugherty to his room at the Huntington Hotel. Empathizing with the frustrated coach, Hannah, according to Daugherty's autobiography, ordered a few beers and said, "Duff, I like to think that the two men sitting in this room right now have done more for the history of Michigan State University than any two men in the history of the school. And I'm not talking about your football coaching, either. You know, there's never been a person who has made more friends for Michigan State than you."

Hannah had an agenda. Tired of losing, Notre Dame was now courting the Irish Catholic Daugherty, just as Texas, USC, and others had done before. The president, sensing danger, wanted a commitment from his coach. "The folks at South Bend want you to coach there next year even if you should lose every game this season," Hannah said. "Now I'm going to speak bluntly. I do not want you to leave Michigan State under any circumstances. I don't want you to go anywhere else. So you tell me, just what will it take to keep you at Michigan State?"

Duffy assured him that it wasn't a matter of money.

The ever-ingenious Hannah then offered the perfect hook. He decided to name Daugherty Director of Football, which made Duffy the sole authority in hiring and firing any football coach, including himself. Duffy Daugherty had the football equivalent of academic tenure. "Now, I've always had considerable respect for my own coaching ability," he wrote, "and I can say in all candor that Duffy the director of football never once contemplated firing Duffy the coach."

In their next game, the Spartans did little to help Daugherty celebrate the Hannah agreement, as 101,450 fans watched their beloved Wolverines tie a 7-7 knot with the Spartans in Ann Arbor. Things looked even worse the next week when the Green and White trailed visiting Indiana 3-0 due to seven fumbles, but State scored on a trick play. Dave McCormick tossed a pass off a fake field goal to fullback Roger Lopes as the Spartans went on to an easy 20-3 win.

Then it was back to Northwestern. The Spartans seemed to own Parseghian's Wildcats. On a delightful football day, 51,013 crowded into Dyche Stadium. The 4-1 NU squad hit first for seven, but in the second half Lewis sailed past the Wildcats for an 87-yard sprint and the Spartans finished the day 15-7 winners.

The 4-1 defending champion Badgers came to East Lansing a week later. The Spartans were down 7-6 when they lost sophomore Juday, who had shown genuine promise as a quarterback, to an injury. Duffy put in Dick Proebstle and hoped for the best. The MSU line stepped up, dominating Wisconsin, and Proebstle led State to three TDs and 30-13 win.

It was an era of big lines, particularly in the Big Ten, so much so that an old story often made the rounds illustrating the phenomenon. A coach was driving through Minnesota, the yarn goes, and encountered an enormous youngster plowing a farm field. When the coach asked the youth for directions to town, the teenaged behemoth picked up the plow and pointed it in the direction of the city. With that, the coach knew he had found another interior lineman for his squad.

The 5-1-1 Spartans, however, had great speed behind their line with Lewis. They also had the nation's best defense, something they demonstrated to Purdue, as the Boilermakers managed just 68 yards on the ground in a 23-0 Spartan victory.

Notre Dame, a team that would win but two games in what would be Joe Kuharich's final season, was next. Duffy and his Catholic players attended mass held at the Student Center prior to the game. The Notre Dame players asked if they could hold their mass at the same time. State politely consented and allowed the visitors to use the center altar. So the two teams held separate services in the same room.

Duffy had invited a friend of his, an Irish priest, to conduct mass at the side altar, while Notre Dame—with, as Daugherty put it, "offensive priests, defensive priests, priests in charge of fumbles and interceptions"—took over the center of the room. At the conclusion of mass, one of the Notre Dame priests informed their squad that he had a relic of St. Bernadette, and invited the players to come forward and kiss it. The uninvited Spartans gawked in silence.

The sly mentor, feeling Notre Dame had tilted the psychological scales unfairly, told his players that the Feast of Our Lady of Lourdes occurred in February, not November, and hence the Fighting Irish were not on the proper blessing schedule. Moreover, the coach explained that Bernadette's sainthood owed largely to her work with the afflicted and that the healthy Spartans should need no special assistance to win.

They almost did. Notre Dame held a 7-6 lead deep into the final period. Then, with less than two minutes left, explosive Sherman Lewis broke loose on an 85-yard gallop for a 12-7 win. Duffy later said, perhaps tongue in cheek, that he had hoped Lewis's speed would not be curtailed by the St. Bernadette medal he had given his back to wear in the contest.

The 12-7 squeaker over Notre Dame on November 16 gave the Spartans a robust 6-1-1 log, 5-0-1 in the conference. The finale on the following Saturday would pit State against powerful 6-1-1 Illinois at East Lansing. A victory would give the Duffy his first Big Ten title and second Rose Bowl trip. On the day before the game, the Spartan players saw an event none would ever forget, the assassination of John F. Kennedy. The Illinois players did not know about the tragedy until their plane landed in East Lansing later in the day. The Spartans, in Duffy's estimation, were heartbroken but aroused, ready to play with zeal and commitment for the president and the nation.

Although the two university presidents agreed to play the contest, as did the NFL on its schedule the following day, Michigan governor George Romney felt otherwise. The game was called off an hour before the kickoff. It would be played five days later.

For the Illini, it was a reprieve. Coach Pete Elliot told Daugherty his team was still in such shock they could not possibly have concentrated effectively on the contest. The Spartans, however, were at such a fever pitch Daugherty took them out on the field for an hour as an outlet for their pent-up energy.

In any case, the Spartans were introduced to one Dick Butkus on that November 28 afternoon. The ferocious center-linebacker smacked Lewis and hammered Lopes, holding the pair to just 91 yards in State's league-leading ground-oriented offense. "Every time I looked up, there *he* was," said Lewis. Butkus, along with seven turnovers—four interceptions and three fumbles—gave the Illini a 13-0 win.

The Spartans had bumbled away the Big Ten championship and their tickets to Pasadena. It was an extremely painful loss for Daugherty, one he attributed largely to the psychological impact of the postponement. "By the time the game got underway the following Thursday, Illinois was high as a kite and our guys couldn't find their fannies with both hands," Daugherty wrote in disgust.

Daugherty had to be delighted at Hannah's creative title and the security that went with it, because the man from Pennsylvania had begun to scour the nation rather than the region in search of talent to wear the Green and White. And he had found it. Phil Hoag, one of the defensive stalwarts of Duffy's 1965 and 1966 teams, recalled his freshman days at MSU. "I remember standing in Jenison [Field House] with the other 60 to 80 freshman," said the Toledo, Ohio, native who went on to become a fast-food magnate in Baltimore. "Duffy was asking who was first team [All-State], who was second team, and half the room was standing at who was first team all-state. We had some tremendous athletes."

One freshman stood out—literally. He was an African American from Beaumont, Texas. "I remember seeing who I thought was the biggest human being on earth, standing there—Charles 'Bubba' Smith," Hoag reminisced. Smith was not the only behemoth. "We were just bigger than everybody else, I mean. Charlie Thornhill just looked like Hercules," said Hoag.

The much-improved Spartans were the best team in the Big Ten in 1963. They led the league in scoring margin (8.6 points per game), rushing (187.2 yards per game), total defense (178.7), and rushing defense (76.2). They outgained their opposition by 93.8 yards per game, by far the best in the league. Sherm Lewis—who, along with end Dan Underwood, was named to the All–Big Ten first team—was #4 in rushing. Lou Bobich led the loop in punting with 41.1 yards per boot, while guard Earl Lattimer and fullback Roger Lopes were second-team all-conference.

The Spartans entered the 1964 season on the heels of five straight winning seasons and a solid 29-14-2 record over that span. The prospects for the coming campaign, however, did not look bright, particularly on offense. The running corps was gone. State figured to rely on stopping their opponents in 1964, with two-way tackles Rahn Bentley and Jerry Rush, linebackers Ron Goovert and Steve Mellinger, and defensive backs Charlie Migyanka and Bobich.

They didn't stop North Carolina in the opener in Tar Heel country. With State keeping a close eye on halfback Ken Willard, Carolina put him in motion in Kenan Stadium, allowing quarterback Danny Talbott to roll out freely. Talbott ran and passed for three scores as the Tar Heels held off rallying MSU 21-15.

The man who could recruit but couldn't coach confounded John McKay's #2 Trojans the following week. Duffy put together a new defense, one in which he pulled a tackle out of the line and replaced him with a fifth secondary man, creating a double-rover effect aimed at stopping USC's sprint-out pass plays and power plays on the ground. After a 49-yard field goal by bare-footed sophomore kicker Dick Kenney, a 2-yard smash by fellow sophomore Clinton Jones, and a TD reception by still another sophomore, Gene Washington (from Harry Ammon), the Spartans had sprung a 17-7 upset. "Just a case of effort transcending ability," said the never-at-a-loss-for-words Daugherty.

The euphoria was short-lived as hated Michigan came in next and pinned a 17-10 loss on the Spartans. With State up 10-9 and only five minutes left in the contest, the Wolverines indulged in a bit of trickery to beat State. Star quarterback Bob Timberlake pitched out to halfback Dick Sygar, who then fired a 31-yard aerial to end John Henderson for the winner.

The 1-2 Spartans then stumbled 27-20 at Indiana, despite junior Steve Juday going 16-20 through the air. By 1964 platoon football was back in full force, after ten years of gradually freer substitution. The result was a more interesting game, one that now included a great deal of passing. In any case, just as the loss to the 0-3 Hoosiers seemed to point to a long season for the Green and White, the Spartans rebounded against Northwestern. A 2-3 Wildcat crew, under new coach Alex Agase, visited East Lansing a week later and left on the short end of a 24-6 verdict.

State then smacked Wisconsin 22-6 in Madison, running its record up to .500. After yielding a first-quarter TD to Purdue's Randy Minniear, the Spartans—running for 302 yards and led by sophomore Jones's two touchdowns—grabbed control of the Boilermakers in East Lansing and won 21-7. Purdue, having knocked the Spartans out of the Rose Bowl picture in 1957 and 1961, felt a similar sting in this one. "We were just repaying the favor," said Daugherty.

Duffy had dominated Ara Parseghian during his days at Northwestern. In fact, prior to State's upcoming game against undefeated Notre Dame, now coached by Parseghian, an MSU adherent boasted, "We'll pluck the magic carpet out from under the Armenian rug peddler." The rug did not move, as Parseghian used a new double-wing offense, one than sprung sophomore star Nick Eddy for 61 yards on the second play. With former Irish coaches Frank Leahy, Hughie Devore, and Terry Brennan looking on, quarterback John Huarte (who would win the Heisman that year) passed for a score and ran 21 yards for another as Notre Dame crushed the Spartans 34-7 in South Bend.

The finale against Illinois would determine whether State finished with a winning or a losing season. With brother Bump of Michigan ready to go to the Rose Bowl, Pete

Elliott's team, led by one-man wrecking crew Butkus on defense and power runner Jim Grabowski, rolled up 185 yards, largely on trap plays, and shut out the Spartans 16-0.

The 1964 squad, having split its six league games, did not really stand out in any important statistical category. Individually, however, Dick Gordon's 571 rushing yards was second-best in the Big Ten, while Steve Juday (5th in passing) led the league with his .564 completion percentage. In addition, the junior threw for seven scores against just four interceptions among his ninety-four attempts. Don Japinga was tops in punt returns (9.4 yards per attempt), while Lou Bobich repeated as punting champ (42 yards per kick). In a season in which the Big Ten picked offensive and defensive all-conference units, Gordon and tackle Jerry Rush were named to the first-team all-league offensive squad. Three players from the secondary—Charlie Migyanka, Herman Johnson, and Japinga—were named on defense, Migyanka to the first and the latter pair to the second team.

Duffy had now completed eleven seasons in East Lansing, four more than his predecessor, Biggie Munn. Eight of those had been winners, and his record, 63-34-3, was more than stellar in an era of parity, particularly in the Big Ten, where he had posted but two losing seasons.

Much sought after both as a coach and celebrity humorist, the man from Barnesboro, Pennsylvania, had much to be happy about, armed with security at Michigan State and regarded as a national leader in his profession. He seemed settled in, but little did he know what was yet to come.

CHAPTER 11

Right Here at Michigan State

**"This team went through the season unbeaten and untied. This is YOUR
team. Now, last year's team won four and lost five. THAT was MY team."**

—Duffy speaking to an alumni group

After a lackluster 1964, Duffy had high hopes for the coming season. The talent supply was richer, and, with a bit more work on the kicking game, he felt a turnaround might be imminent. In preseason doubles, Daugherty emphasized all aspects of the kicking game, from field goals to fake field goals to onside kicks, never tiring of reminding his team that more contests are determined by the kicking game than any other aspect of football.

Two nights before the opener, during the team's regular Thursday dinner meeting, Daugherty asked one of his players, "Where are most football games lost?"

"Right here at Michigan State," was the youth's instant reply.

The kicking did improve, however, much due to the barefoot Hawaiian Dick Kenney, who booted eleven field goals. In the Michigan game, the snap went awry on the thirty and Kenney picked up the ball and began scurrying around this way and that, not knowing what to do. Daugherty feared twin disasters—that he might be thrown for an excessive loss and that he might injure his foot in the process. Later he told Kenney that should such an event occur again, he should simply drop-kick the ball. If it went through, State would get 3 points. If it missed, it would be a touchback and the opposition would get the ball on the twenty.

Then Duffy topped it off with what had to be an apocryphal story. He told of a Thanksgiving Day game back in Barnesboro when his team had the ball on the Spangler eight-yard line and the coach told Daugherty to try a field goal. Of course, the snap was bad, but through Duffy's wizardry he got control of the ball and drop-kicked it through the uprights. "It still stands out as one of my greatest thrills in football," he chortled. "It didn't even matter that we lost the game 69-3."

The Spartans were not on the 1965 Big Ten radar screen. Observers had them behind Michigan (slotted for 8th in the country by *Sports Illustrated*), Purdue, Ohio State, Iowa, and Minnesota. A mirthful Duffy joined in the badmouthing. "Last year we had a wide-open passing game, broke every record in Michigan State history, and lost all our Big Ten games," he said fancifully. "This year we'll run and throw one long incomplete pass every game just to loosen up our opposition."

The wily coach knew he had some face cards to play in 1965. That 1963 treasure trove of talent was now in its third year, among a number of other quality players. There was quarterback Steve Juday (seventy-nine completions for 879 yards), running back Clinton Jones (350 yards rushing), end Gene Washington, and Hawaiian-native fullback Bob Apisa, to lead the ever-changing multiple offense. Barefoot placekicker Dick Kenney, another Hawaiian, gave the Spartans additional punch. On the other side of the ball stood Bubba Smith and Harold Lucas on the line, with Ron Goovert and Charlie Thornhill backing them.

The Spartans opened the campaign with a nondescript 13-3 win over the UCLA Bruins in East Lansing. At the time, little was made of the win, but by season's end it loomed large, as UCLA would finish the regular season with a 7-2-1 log. Moreover, the Bruins' inability to register more than a field goal was a harbinger of things to come for Spartan opponents. Nonetheless, at the time it was just a win, and a good way to get started.

A lackluster (5-5 on the season as an independent playing second-tier competition) Penn State eleven was next. Duffy's defense posted a shutout in Happy Valley as State rolled over the Nittany Lions 23-0. Despite the team's 2-0 start, no one seemed to be taking notice. The Spartans were the stepchild of the state of Michigan, and Bob Griese was grabbing all the headlines for the undefeated Boilermakers.

Soon the Big Ten had only one team standing with an unblemished record, as Georgia topped Michigan 15-7 and SMU hung a 14-14 stalemate on Purdue. That team was Duffy Daugherty's surprising Spartans, who put down the Illini 22-12 in East Lansing. "We haven't really exploited our passing yet," said Duffy, wholly tongue in cheek. What Duffy intended to exploit were the Illini's sophomore ends. Led by future Green Bay Packer Jim Grabowski and quarterback Fred Custardo, Illinois jumped out to an early 10-3 edge. The score was 12-9 late in the third when what appeared to be the gamebreaker occurred. Grabowski broke away for what looked like a certain clinching TD only to have defensive back Jim Summers trip him up with a dive at midfield, saving the game. Then the Spartan machine fired up and Clinton Jones went in from 13 yards out, followed by Bob Apisa from 10 yards away, and Michigan State had restored order to the tune of 15-12. A Steve Juday to Gene Washington aerial completed the scoring.

Juday was emerging as the team's offensive leader. Hailing from tiny (pop. 4,000) Northville, Michigan, the handsome signal-caller who impressed at least one teammate as the kind of guy one would "tear down the walls" for, was an A student in marketing and a member of the Excalibur, a campus honor society. Though lacking the arm to be a pro prospect, according to scouts, Juday was the unquestioned offensive leader. He had Daugherty's complete confidence, as the coach allowed the highly intelligent youngster to call 90% of the team's plays. Juday had presence, a sort of detached air, an attractive aloofness that made him the leader. He would chew out teammates for missed blocks and tolerate no nonsense in the huddle. "He is not the type you give a hotfoot to," said one player.

Despite the jelling of the team, people were not yet buying in to Duffy's charges. Although MSU was perfect through three games and had outscored opponents by a combined 58-15, *Sports Illustrated* still had the Spartans behind the 2-0-1 Boilermakers in the Midwest.

Moreover, the next three weeks would determine whether the Spartans were contenders or pretenders, as State would play Michigan in Ann Arbor, followed by Ohio State at home, and then mighty Purdue in West Lafayette. Line coach Hank Bullough later said, "Every day in September when I'd see that schedule on the back of the scoreboard at home I'd break out in a sweat. Penn State, Michigan, Ohio State . . . 'Just no way,' I'd say to myself. 'No way.'" Despite having disposed of their first three foes, it was reasonable to assume that Duffy's charges would be 3-3 by the final week of October.

Thirsting for recognition and revenge, the Spartans headed to Ann Arbor for their annual collision with hated Michigan. A crowd of 103,219 looked on in dismay as Duffy's charges hammered the Wolverines, 24-7. The enormous yet mobile Spartan linemen, led by 286-pound defensive end Bubba Smith, 268-pound middle guard Harold Lucas, and 218-pound rover George Webster, led the vaunted 5-3 defense, swamping would-be Michigan runners and holding the Wolverines to −39 yards on the ground. Quarterback Dick Vidmer ran for cover amid the jailbreak State rush, becoming a virtual postage stamp on the Ann Arbor turf. The defense also covered two Wolverine bobbles. On offense, Juday, Jones, and Apisa crossed the goal for the Spartans. *Sports Illustrated* now took notice and moved Michigan State to the #2 position in the Midwest, behind only Nebraska.

A letdown was possible now, as the Spartans, fresh from their high in Ann Arbor, would face Woody Hayes's Buckeyes at home. "You know these fellows have yet to reach their full potential," said Daugherty with uncharacteristic optimism as State delivered a 32-7 pummeling of Ohio State, a team that would not lose a single 1965 conference contest save for this one. The one-sided nature of the game was evident early, when the mighty D of the Spartans put Buckeye quarterback Don Unverferth down in his own end zone for a safety and a 12-0 lead. Before the carnage was over, the Spartans had held Ohio State to −22 yards rushing, while piling up a whopping 538 yards on total offense themselves. Juday's leadership was in particular evidence in the win, as he would call the play in the huddle but not signal in which direction it would go until after he got to the line of scrimmage and ascertained the placement of the Buckeye roverback. Running away from the roverback game-long made the Spartans almost unstoppable. One who ran away was Clinton Jones. He scored twice, once on an 80-yard sprint. Bob Apisa rung up his fifth TD of the campaign and barefoot placekicker Dick Kenney hit on his ninth field goal. Michigan State now ranked second in the nation.

Jones was a feel-good story in 1965. Called by some the closest thing to Jim Brown, the 6'1" 208-pound dynamo had no weaknesses on the gridiron. He had a driving, tackle-breaking running style, yet could be gone if he got but a step on a defender. Juday wisely exploited Jones's skills, often sending lanky Gene Washington—who would draw double coverage—deep to clear an area in which he would hit Jones with a strike. He would also reverse the play, lofting an aerial to Washington when he got only single coverage. Off the field, Jones became a member of the Big Brother Society and worked diligently with a troubled Lansing youngster. Meeting with him four nights a week, Jones inspired the young man to clean up his life. "The first thing he did was get a haircut," related Jones. "He really straightened up and even started going to church. Before each game he would tell me that he was going to pray for me and the team not to get hurt. Nothing I've done has been as rewarding to me as helping that boy."

The game of the season now awaited, as the Spartans headed for Purdue to face the 4-0-1 Boilers. Boilermaker fans expected to win as frat houses were adorned with banners stating, "Everything's Coming Up Roses!" and "Here Lie the Rose Bowl Dreams of MSU, Died on the Day They Met Purdue." Nevertheless, *Sports Illustrated* picked Duffy's men in a squeaker, stating, "State's fierce defense will stop Griese's passes."

They didn't, at least in the first half. On a blustery, overcast day, in front of a homecoming throng of 62,113, Griese opened the scoring with a 20-yard field goal and followed that with a TD capping an incredible 96-yard drive for a 10-0 lead at the break. Griese, operating behind an unbalanced line installed by Coach Jack Mollenkopf for just this game, hit thirteen of his passes in the first half, eight to ace split end Bob Hadrick. It looked as if the uniforms had been switched on the other side of the line, as it was Purdue that showed the defensive dominance in this confrontation.

With a gale wind dominating play, such that before the game Purdue's Jack Mollenkopf kidded with Daugherty, suggesting that each team's offense should have the wind advantage all day, while having to punt into the howitzer.

Michigan State focused on field position in the second half. It was in the third quarter that the nor'wester wreaked havoc on Mollenkopf's team. State forced Purdue's all-everything Bob Griese to punt four times into the wind. Griese's boots traveled an average of 22.5 yards, with his longest being a 30-yarder. Moreover the Spartan field position strategy worked, such that State ran only six of its sixty-five second-half offensive plays on State's side of the field. In fact, Purdue never moved beyond its own forty-two in the third quarter, its own 25 in the fourth. The Boilermakers had six possessions in the second half, five of which were started at or inside their own 20.

The Spartans took over five times inside Purdue territory. The grinding down effect of this disadvantage was gradual but cumulative for Purdue, finally evidencing itself in the fourth quarter when the State ground game really kicked in. With Apisa and Jones running inside rather than outside Purdue's tough end Jim Long, the two tore away at the tired Boiler defense behind gap blocks by the Spartan line. Michigan State mounted a 50-yard drive that ended with Apisa crashing over from an inch out.

Duffy, never going for the tie, ordered up a two-point conversion pass. It worked and the score was 10-8, but with nine minutes and forty-six seconds left and the wind now favoring Purdue.

Two plays then turned the game. The first occurred on the ensuing kickoff, when the Purdue return man collided with a teammate and went down on his own 9-yard line. With the Boilermakers too far into their own kitchen to throw, Griese stayed on the ground in what became a three and out. Although his punt did carry to midfield, Drake Garrett ran it back to the Purdue 39. Purdue's defense was now flagging, having played nearly the entire second half with their backs against the field position wall, and State took advantage. Apisa and Jones began bashing through the defense and picked up a first down. The drive appeared stopped, however, when Juday missed on a third-down aerial at the 22. With the wind howling in State's face, a field goal attempt, even by the estimable Dick Kenney, seemed an unlikely success. But there was more to the failed pass play than initially met the eye. The flag on the field was the clue. A Purdue defensive end had bumped into Juday after the whistle, and the call was roughing the passer, with State setting up shop on the Boilermaker 12. Several plays later Jones followed some thunderous blocks by Apisa and guard John Karpinski, scoring from 8 yards out, and the game belonged to the Spartans.

Purdue did not recover quickly from the devastating loss as their 21-0 defeat at the hands of a middling Illini team the following week attests. As for this one, however, the Spartan defense simply overpowered the Boilermakers in the second half. Griese completed but two throws for a meager 14 yards. He finished the game with six straight incompletions. Much of the credit belonged to the Spartans' defensive captain, 5'8" 164-pound Don Japinga. Japinga, also a member of the prestigious Excalibur, walked on as a freshman but had become so adept at secondary play that Daugherty matched him up man-to-man against some of the best receivers the Spartans encountered. Purdue's 6'2" Hadrick had Japinga for lunch in the first half, and the diminutive Spartan was enraged. The first time he could get close to the Purdue end after the break, Japinga laid down the gauntlet. "Hadrick, you won't catch another one today," he declared. Japinga was off by just one reception, and that one was for but 6 yards.

Asked about the secret ingredients of his team's success, Daugherty listed enthusiasm and a willingness to reach for their potential, along with, "of course, some excellent coaching." Though he may have been kidding about the latter, all three were in evidence. Assistant coach Bullough was amazed at the enthusiasm and the willingness of the squad to stretch themselves. Players regularly came into his office to ask questions, often leaving with a film of one of the games for further study. The defensive regulars lifted together and added over 100 pounds of raw muscle from the previous year. "I think they felt they got pushed around by the other boys in the league a little too much last year," said Daugherty.

The coaching staff, however, was earning its pay. Good players were becoming great players, and an ignored team was now a national power. They had also helped to forge a tremendous team unity and commitment. No one let up. End Bob Viney played on a bad knee but pressed on, ignoring the pain. "They see him limping around making tackles," said Bullough, "and they know they haven't the right to loaf. And they're all the time correcting each other, sometimes in no uncertain terms. Man, they *yell* at one another." In any organization, you know the corner has turned when the norm becomes excellence and the group organ rejects slackers. Michigan State had turned the corner, and it was exhilarating.

"I love these guys," said a euphoric Japinga. "This team just makes you love everyone on it. I just can't believe this is happening to us. It's wonderful, but I just can't believe it."

Purdue did believe it. When a Spartan fan raised a green-and-white flag after the game and declared, "There'll be joy in Mudville!" an unhappy Purdue adherent had the perfect response. "That's what you think, mister. *This* is Mudville."

Now 6-0 (4-0 in the league), State now faced the softer side of the Big Ten schedule—three teams that would finish a combined 7-23 for the season. Northwestern was first, and the home Spartans declawed the Wildcats to the tune of 49-7. Holding Northwestern to 7 rushing yards, Apisa struck for his 7th, 8th, and 9th TDs of the season, leaving defeated Wildcat coach Alex Agase to remark in awe of the Spartans, "One of the finest teams I've ever seen. They're too big to run on, they don't give you much time to pass, and I've never seen backs run with such power." The only regret many national football followers had was that State would not meet Nebraska that year, so no one could be quite sure who had the better team.

For Duffy, life was good, and he milked every ounce of its goodness, all the while spreading the magic of Spartan football. In an anonymous internet article, "Why I Love Michigan State Football," the author dates his devotion to the Spartans back to 1965, when as a twelve-year-old member of a Boy Scout troop he volunteered as an usher at Spartan Stadium. Once down on the field with his troopmaster father, the youth had a magic moment with the now bigger-than-life coach. He watched Duffy "place his hand on my dad's shoulder and shake his hand. He then shook the hand of each of us and when he got to me he smiled at all of us and had that wink in his eye, and said, 'Boys, we are going to have some fun today!'

"And boy did we have fun! It was 1965, a time when giants walked the earth. And they held high court at Spartan Stadium. We called them Bubba or Washington or Webster or Mad Dog [Thornhill]. When they ran out of the north tunnel the ground shook and the crowd roared. Many teams were afraid to face these giants and rightly so, as they turned out to be one of the greatest teams in college to play the game."

The giants of State clinched a tie for the Big Ten crown the following week in Iowa City, destroying the Hawkeyes, 35-0. "Don't forget," said Daugherty in typical curmudgeon fashion, "you have to be voted into the Rose Bowl (by the Big Ten)." State closed the conference season against a lowly Indiana squad at East Lansing. Having outscored their previous six conference opponents by a combined 176-43 (an average roughly of 30-7), Spartan faithful settled back ready to enjoy a full-scale rout of the hapless Hoosiers.

With less than a quarter remaining, paradise was in peril of being lost, as Indiana led, 13-10. The concerned throng then got its reprieve as Steve Juday hit Gene Washington twice—once for 43 yards—for TDs and Dick Kenney kicked his second field goal to give the Spartans a 17-point fourth quarter, and a decisive 27-13 triumph. In all Washington caught three TDs in the contest.

There was, however, one game left. It pitted the Spartans against mighty Notre Dame in South Bend. The Irish, who fell an upset short of a national championship in 1964, were coming into this one with a gaudy 7-1-1 mark. The day was clear, cold, and windy, with sixty thousand people in attendance, some having paid $100 for their ticket. The first half appeared tailor-made for the Irish, as they got the ball on State's 19, 25, and 18-yard lines, due to the generosity of the Spartan offense. But the Irish did not take advantage of the State largesse. Tom Longo made a diving interception of a Juday aerial at the 25, only to have linebacker Charlie Thornhill return the compliment against the Irish. A few minutes later, Juday fumbled on the 18, but Don Japinga picked off a would-be TD toss in the end zone. In short, the Irish managed only a Ken Ivan field goal, making the halftime score 3-0.

Late in the third quarter, State took control. Starting on Notre Dame's 39, Clinton Jones—who would gain 117 yards on the ground for the game—ripped off 21 yards, and four plays later he and Dwight Lee had gotten down to the three. Then, with what looked like USC's famed student body right, Jones rumbled into the end zone and the lead was State's for keeps. Scoring was completed in the fourth quarter on a Juday-to-Lee touchdown toss.

It was a bruising defensive battle in a year in which offenses exploded around the nation. The game included seventeen punts, five interceptions, and twenty-nine rushing plays that yielded no or negative yardage. Michigan State had the better of it, holding the Irish to –12 rushing yards, something that no one could remember ever happening before. Notre Dame tried to pass because the Irish could not run against State's mobile 5-3 defense. When Notre Dame ran to the right, they met an unfriendly 6'7" Bubba Smith. When they moved left, it was Bob Viney. When they tried to go inside, they faced linebackers Ron Goovert, Buddy Owens, and Charlie Thornhill, along with 6'4" roverback George Webster.

Home or road, the 1965 team seemed to get stronger and more flexible as the game wore on. This contest marked State's sixth come-from-behind win. For the season, the Spartans had outscored their opponents 103-7 in the final quarter.

Although the savvy defense, plus the late offensive adjustments, reinstalled Daugherty as an X's and O's wizard—after becoming better known as a humorist—the mentor couldn't help but quip, "You might say we were a second half team." Explanations for the Spartans' surprising prowess abounded. Some attributed it to Juday's leadership. Others felt Clinton Jones, who gained 787 yards on the ground through the ten-game season, made State tough all by himself. Still others cited the team's confidence. Duffy, however, pointed to conditioning, coachability, and commitment, adding as only he could, "We seem to be off to our best start in years."

Accolades came from far and wide for this national team. In an era of local recruiting, State had three players from South Carolina and three from Texas, in addition to others from Virginia, Pennsylvania, and Hawaii. Although the AP would await the bowl results, the UPI crowned the Spartans the 1965 national champions. Indeed, the best football in the country had been played "right here at Michigan State."

Most football observers felt about the Spartans as did one Big Ten scribe in this Vietnam era. "They come in waves, like Chinese communists. The only thing they don't do is beat on garbage-can tops with bayonets." They certainly beat on the Big Ten. On offense, they led the league in rushing, total offense, and scoring. On defense, they were even better, permitting a simply unbelievable 34.6 yards per game on the ground and a mere 181.7 overall, to go with but 56 points. Individually, Jones and Apisa ranked #2 and #3 in conference game rushing, with Juday third in passing. Jones won the scoring title with 68 points, with Apisa fourth at 44. Gene Washington's 544 receiving yards placed him #2 in the conference, while Drake Garrett's 11.6 average on punt returns was the Big Ten's best. Eight players—Gene Washington, Steve Juday, Clinton Jones, Charles (Bubba) Smith, Harold Lucas, Ron Goovert, George Webster, and Don Japinga—made either the AP or UPI All–Big Ten first team. Four more—offensive tackle Jerry West, guard John Karpinski, center Boris Dimitroff, and Apisa—were named to a second team. Juday, Japinga, and tackle Dan Bierowicz were named to the All-Academic unit.

Duffy could not have felt better or been more witty. "The secret of this team is that our sophomores and juniors haven't had the full benefit of my coaching," he said with typical self-deprecation.

Their Rose Bowl opponent was an upstart UCLA bunch, a team State defeated 13-3 in the season opener. With the Spartans a two-touchdown favorite, some felt Tommy Prothro's 8-2-1 Bruins would be fortunate to leave Pasadena intact after facing the all-conquering Spartans. "Michigan State is the best team in the country," *Sports Illustrated* stated unequivocally, "and is better now than it was when it beat UCLA 13-3 in September." The Uclans were led by sophomore quarterback sensation Gary Beban, who had rolled up over 1,900 yards running and passing his team to a Rose Bowl bid thanks to his clutch performance in a 20-16 upset of archrival USC. He was UCLA's only hope, but then so was Bob Griese for Purdue. "A combination of these circumstances—a good day for Beban and a mediocre day for the Spartans—probably would result in a UCLA upset," opined *Sports Illustrated*. "But let us be realistic," it went on. "What is more likely to occur is at least a fair day for the Spartans and something less than a sensational performance by Gary Beban. In this case, Michigan State would win by the two touchdowns the bookmakers foresee."

Although Tommy Prothro was better known for creative strategizing than intense work habits, he employed both in preparation for this confrontation. After two weeks of confidence-instilling practices, the tall Southerner remarked, "I've just about mesmerized myself into thinking we can win." On game day, Prothro felt prepared. "We're ready," he said down on the field. "We're gone try to swarm 'em."

Before there was any swarmin', the Bruins needed an offensive game plan. Prothro realized he could not go belly-to-belly with State. To do so was to look down the barrel of a blowout. "We decided that was no use tryin' to get at Michigan State with anything but unorthodox tools," he related in retrospect. "We gone all the way with the bomb. When it's third and one or third and two, don't look for us to run for the first down." Furthermore, Prothro installed what he called the shadow set, an alignment in which his two top receivers—Dick Witcher and Kurt Altenburg—lined up on the same side of the field, one in front of the other. "With this," the coach explained, "we could seep toward our strength. If they overshifted, we could run away from it. And if they closed up quickly we could throw long to Witcher or Altenburg."

True to his word, Prothro's charges used an unorthodox tactic on its first offensive play. Beban faked from the shadow and rumbled across the field for 28 stunning yards. Although it did not eventuate in a score, the maneuver had an inspiring effect. "It gave us confidence, and gave them the hint we could run on them," said Beban. UCLA's offense kicked in the second quarter, with the first TD requiring no trick plays. A Spartan fumble was quite sufficient. Daugherty had long made it a cardinal principle that no punt be received inside the ten. Apparently, he had not made it cardinal enough, because a Bruin boot lofting through the California skies had the State kick returner backing up to grab it, only leaving a bobbled pigskin under a Uclan jersey at the Green and White five. Beban eventually pushed it over from the one to make it 7-0. The Spartans were undaunted, having trailed in six of their previous ten wins, and readied themselves for a game-tying drive. It didn't happen.

Duffy realized that Prothro might reach his Merlin arm into his bag of tricks now that he had State down and try an onside kick. More specifically, he believed it would go to UCLA's left and the Spartans' right. Daugherty warned his troops to be alert for a short boot, but apparently not sternly enough. The Bruins executed the maneuver successfully and set up in the shadow alignment once again. With the two ace receivers split wide, Beban's "shadow set Michigan, spread left post" call sent the pair crisscrossing en route to the end zone. Beban sent a spiral to Altenburg, who was pulled down a yard short of the goal. From there, Beban smashed over for a 14-0 lead.

A crowd of 100,087 fans watched with amazement as the swarmin' Bruins shut out the mighty Spartans through three quarters. Nothing was certain, however, because the men from Michigan State, sultans of the fourth quarter, had owned the final fifteen minutes all season long, having outscored their opposition by nearly 100 points over the campaign. Indeed, the Spartans awakened. Powerful Bob Apisa raced 38 yards for State's initial score, making it 14-6. Duffy was not interested in a tie, so he went for two, realizing that if he made it and scored again, a regular PAT would give State the win. If he failed, well then a late-game two-pointer behind a score could still get him a deadlock. The Spartans didn't make it, and the season was ticking away. With the clock UCLA's best friend, it appeared the packed Rose Bowl would be the venue of the day's biggest bowl upset. But with just 38 seconds left, State scored, making it 14-12, UCLA.

The issue was joined. Either the goliaths from the Big Ten would power over for 2 points and a tie, or UCLA would complete the shocker. Bruins fans hardly dared to hope, while State fans wondered what Duffy would call. The ball went Bob Apisa, who took a lateral and rumbled around right end. Bruin co-captain and end Jim Colletto wrestled Apisa around the head, but the human bull kept on pushing for the stripe. Linebacker Dallas Grider aided Colletto, but Apisa was not to be denied. As he plunged for the goal, defensive back Bob Stiles, hurled all his 5'9" 175 pounds headfirst into Apisa's side. The cataclysmic collision resulted in Stiles having to helped off the field, but more important, it sent Apisa crashing to the Rose Bowl turf, just two feet short of pay dirt.

Game MVP Stiles was the defensive leader all day long, as the gnat-like Bruin defense indeed swarmed around Spartan ballcarriers. In addition, Stiles picked off two passes, thwarting a pair of State drives.

Although a tie would have been less than satisfying, given that Bear Bryant's Alabama Crimson Tide upended mighty Nebraska, and LSU downed similarly undefeated Arkansas, failure to convert on the end run may well have cost the Spartans the AP national championship. A crestfallen and outcoached Daugherty, who would later remark, "It's bad luck to be behind at the end of the game," mustered grace if not humor in verbally rendering with pinpoint accuracy the day's gridiron obituary. "They kept us off balance from the start," said the fifty-year-old mentor.

Clearly the Spartans had gotten drunk on their press clippings. "We really thought we were the 'jolly green giants,'" Daugherty later lamented, "but we played like mice for three quarters." The team had not been emotionally prepared, and Duffy was helpless to do anything about it. True to Vince Lombardi's belief that most games are lost rather than won, the unfocused Spartans committed five turnovers in the defeat.

Daugherty did not go back to East Lansing after the game. He tried to unwind, playing golf with his old Stanford friend, Jack Curtice in Santa Barbara. He had hardly put the clubs back in the bag before he was hospitalized with a rare virus. There he received a telegram from the university board of trustees. It read, "We wish you a speedy recovery, by a vote of four to three."

CHAPTER 12

At the Summit

"Football is not a contact sport. Football is a collision sport. Dancing is a contact sport."

mbarrassed, angry, and humiliated, Spartan fans were not without hope after the 1965 comedown. Although the team was ineligible for the Rose Bowl the following year due to the Big Ten's no-repeat rule, the 1966 season was but nine months away. And with the likes of Smith, Webster, Thornhill, Washington, Apisa, Jones, and Kenney returning, a loss like this figured to goad Michigan State into another national championship run, an even more single-minded, tunnel-vision effort, aimed at completing the unfinished business of 1965.

The Spartans would sneak up on no one in 1966, and Hugh Daugherty knew it. Picked as the Big Ten's best in most quarters, State was trying to accomplish something only the 1955 Ohio State team had done over the past fifteen years, repeat as conference champions. In fact, the average finish for defending champions was fifth. "Sure, there's something to it," the genial mentor allowed. "The lack of the Rose Bowl incentive is a real thing, and I am not naïve enough to think we can be an automatic winner. After all, we did lose the heart of our defense (Lucas, tackle Buddy Owens, Bierowicz, Goovert, and Viney). But we'll survive, and we'll be hard for anyone to beat."

The professional pigskin observers agreed. Michigan State was a certain top ten team nationally in their minds and might well duel for the national championship that had gotten away on New Year's Day. Offensively, the Spartans were loaded. Washington, who doubled as the Big Ten hurdles champion, had pulled in 40 passes for 638 yards the previous season. Linemen Jerry West and Joe Przbycki were solid performers. Moreover, the Jones-Apisa-Lee triumvirate had rolled up over 1,800 yards in '65. Apisa, however, was recovering from knee surgery, and his status was not certain. Then there was Dick Kenney, the much-heralded barefoot Hawaiian returned having tallied 53 points a season ago.

The team may well have been tabbed to win it all were it not for one huge question mark: the quarterback position. The absence of three-year starter Steve Juday left a gaping hole. Juday was clearly one of the principal reasons for State's 1965 success. Moreover, Juday had been the team's leader and galvanizing force of intelligence and commitment that championship teams need to remain focused. His replacement was an untested 5'10" speedster named Jimmy Raye.

Even more important in an era of burning cities, an emerging Black Power movement, and general racial tension, Raye was African American. A black man would be leading the Green and White charges in 1966, a black man who—only a junior—had no experience under center at the college level and whose passing skills were suspect at best, a black man who therefore would give State the one thing its offense did not need, more running capacity. So much of Michigan State's offensive success, one that netted the team over 26 points a game in 1965, owed to Juday's wizardry, more specifically his ability to confuse defenses by mixing unexpected aerials with the team's punishing ground game.

A poorly kept secret throughout the decades is that African American athletes have long been regarded as physical freaks, people with uncommon jumping and sprinting skills, but short on intellectual acumen. Racist as this canard is, it has stood up against incredible evidence to the contrary. The new millennium arrived with still many white fans stubbornly adhering to this nonsense. In 1966 this racist doctrine was so prevalent it was not assailed. In fact it was not mentioned. It was accepted as fact, and no one could possibly have been more familiar with it than Raye, who was from Fayetteville, North Carolina. In a word, Jimmy Raye was in what appeared to be a no-win position. If he won, well that was expected. If he didn't, the difference would be attributed to the absence of Mr. Dean's List himself, Steve Juday. To Daugherty's credit, however, he did not do the politically safe if not correct thing: find a white youth, any white youth, who could loft an occasional pass when he wasn't handing off to Jones, Lee, and Apisa. Jimmy Raye, an intellectually gifted young man who went on to a distinguished career constructing offenses for championship NFL teams, was Duffy's man, and so he would be The Man for the mighty Green and White.

One of Daugherty's finest traits is that in matters of principle he did not much care what others thought. Further, he had no illusions as to his ability to alter attitudes and transform the character of others. Daugherty's explication of his character/values distinction in his rather scholarly 1961 book, *1st and Ten*, he wrote with educator Clifford B. Wilson, is telling. "Misconceptions frequently arise regarding the educational values of competitive athletics," he wrote. "It is certain that athletics provide opportunities for the development of 'character.' They abound with circumstances favorable to the development of sociological concepts necessary for adequate democratic living: understanding of competition, cooperation, leadership, 'followership'; respect for authority; respect for people, regardless of race, color, or creed; sportsmanlike conduct. These endless values are purely potential at best, however."

Here, however, he drew a sharp line. He stated that the values he taught were "to be absorbed, ignored or rejected by the individual participant." Nothing was guaranteed when it came to people learning and doing the right thing simply because they are confronted with matters of value. "Each individual will react negatively or positively, depending upon his personal nature and the environmental forces surrounding him." Daugherty may as well have been writing about the internalization of the values of fairness and equal opportunity in the general population as he was about the lessons learned in athletics. Daugherty had learned that people will do and believe what they want to do and believe. He could lead horses to the water of open-mindedness and equal treatment, he could do and teach the right thing in the face of resistance, but he could not change people's hearts and minds.

As much as whites may have recoiled at the sight of a black field general, African American students took note of the coach's pioneering ways. One of them was Philip Hart, director of the Trotter Institute for the Study of Black Culture at the University of Massachusetts–Boston. "I was reminded of the historic role of athletics and academics at MSU in a recent *New York Times* article," he wrote in the UMass-Boston *University Reporter* thirty-seven years later. "I was at that game [against Notre Dame], during my first year in graduate school at MSU, where football was king. All the talk was about players like Bubba Smith, Jimmy Raye, George Webster and the coach who brought these southern boys to MSU, Duffy Daugherty. These black players, who were from Texas, North Carolina, and South Carolina, were not yet welcome at the predominantly white universities in their home states. So they migrated north to Michigan seeking their athletic fortunes. As the *Times* article notes, Daugherty was one of the first coaches to create a nucleus of black stars at a school like MSU. At the time Notre Dame only had one black player, Alan Page, who is now a Supreme Court justice in Minnesota."

Amid this pride and prejudice, the season began.

A very average (5-5 for the season) North Carolina State team provided the opposition in the opener in East Lansing, and the Spartans disposed of the Wolfpack handily, 28-10, behind the devastating running of Jones and Apisa, with the former picking up 129 yards on 19 carries. Daugherty had wisely adjusted his offense to accommodate the elusive Raye. He used Raye on the option and put in a balanced line to augment the speedy quarterback's style. Always looking for the edge, the wily Irishman planted a caveat for opponents, saying, "That doesn't mean we won't be unbalanced in the fall." The skinny quarterback was one of a number of smaller players in comparison to 1965, necessitating Duffy's alteration in approach. "We like our offense carefree but not irresponsible," he explained. "We know we can't blow people out of there with power anymore, so we'll rely more upon surprise and speed."

The Spartans did blow out their week-two opponent, however, pounding Joe Paterno's Nittany Lions by a lopsided 42-8 margin in East Lansing. Raye had his coming-out party, tossing a pair of TDs to Gene Washington, one going 50 yards, while Bob Apisa and Clinton Jones added three more scores between them. Paterno was awestruck as the Spartans walloped his squad with bravado. "We just stood around and let them taunt us," he remarked. "It was our fault, not theirs."

The 2-0 start against nonconference competition was worthy of note. The Big Ten had slipped noticeably over the past four seasons, going 15-7, 14-10, 13-13, and now just 11-14 against teams from rival conferences. Crusty Woody Hayes downplayed nonloop games, referring to them as exhibitions. Duffy, however, needing every win possible in quest of a national championship, saw it differently. "I take them all seriously," he stated. He had done so for a long time. An "advanced thinker among Big Ten coaches," according to *Sports Illustrated*, Daugherty had posted a solid 29-7 record against non–Big Ten competition. The Big Ten was at a disadvantage, however, as it did not permit redshirting. Perhaps more important, the Midwest was no longer regarded as the haven for high school football talent. To Daugherty's credit, he saw a leveling off coming and adjusted by recruiting nationally. Bubba Smith was from Beaumont, Texas, with fellow Lone Star State native Gene Washington hailing from LaPorte. George Webster was from Anderson, South Carolina. Of course, Raye, Apisa, and Kenney also came from far out of the Midwest.

More important, however, is that Smith, Webster, Raye, and Washington were all African Americans out of the South, where they were as yet unwelcome on many state campuses. This gave Duffy the edge. As *Sports Illustrated* put it, "Equality is here, and the proud old Big Ten must live with it. If Duffy Daugherty and Bubba Smith will just cooperate."

Despite the impressive start, there were many who did not feel State was the best even in the Midwest. Not even second best. For many, Notre Dame and Nebraska, the rulers of the Great Plains, were State's superiors. The Spartans again would have no opportunity to settle matters with the Cornhuskers, given that Nebraska was not on their schedule and State was not eligible for bowl play, having been to Pasadena, the Big Ten's only bowl venue, the previous season. The Green and White would, however, get a crack at Ara Parseghian's Fighting Irish. In fact, from the outset of the season, fans of both teams marked off the weeks carefully in hopes that the two might remain undefeated as they entered what would figure to be a simply colossal November 19 date in East Lansing.

But that was far in the future and the Big Ten schedule now awaited. An 0-2 Illinois team, minus its top runner, Cyril Pinder, out with knee surgery, was first. Coach Pete Elliott, in the Prothro tradition, used wider formations, more passing, and a man in motion to spread the State linebackers. Not to be outdone, Duffy countered with a 4-4-2-1 prevent defense, as Bubba Smith and company held the Illini to 17 yards rushing. Although Illinois harnessed Apisa and Jones, Michigan State showed its offensive versatility in prevailing 26-10 in Champaign-Urbana. Dwight Lee ran for a 10-yard score, and 220-pound guard Pat Gallinagh realized every lineman's dream. He took a lateral from end Phil Hoag, who had snared a fumble in midair—one of three recoveries for Hoag—and ground his way downfield 40 yards for a TD. Raye, who delivered another 50-yard strike to Gene Washington, contributed a three-yard scoring run, while sophomore Al Brenner ran a punt back 95 yards for yet another score. Despite the win, Daugherty was not pleased. "They forced us into mistakes," he moaned.

It was the best of times and the most tense of times for the coach. On one hand, he had what he so desperately wanted, a truly great, championship-level team. On the other, he was now the hunted, with wins generating more relief than euphoria. Not losing was eclipsing winning in importance.

Fortunately, the team's next foe, archrival Michigan, would be coming to East Lansing this year. The Spartans crushed the Wolverines for the second consecutive year, this time, 20-7. Michigan could not run and knew it. Quarterback Dick Vidmer tried to compensate by throwing forty-seven times, but to little avail as he completed just thirteen passes. It was not an artistic effort on either side, as the contest was tarnished by eight fumbles and thirteen penalties. Nonetheless, the Spartans were now 4-0 and heading into Columbus to play a grimly determined Buckeye team that had uncharacteristically lost two straight.

Woody Hayes had his gridiron gang ready and 82,282 howling adherents roared their encouragement to the Buckeyes in the famed "Horseshoe." With State leading 3-0 on a Dick Kenney field goal, Ohio State moved ahead 8-3 on a 47-yard strike from Bill Long to Billy Anders. Staring in the face of possible defeat and the obliteration of any championship hopes, Raye directed his teammates, much due to his own running and passing, on an 82-yard drive for a first down on the Buckeye two. There the smashing was even more intense, as Ohio State denied the Spartans on their first three attempts. With everything on the line, State gave the ball to Bob Apisa, and this time the mighty fullback did not repeat the Rose Bowl scenario. He slammed over to put State up 9-8.

Duffy needed two for his team to have any breathing room at all. He got it, as Dick Kenney faked the PAT and threw to his holder, Charley Wedemeyer, for the conversion. Ohio State, however, was not finished. With 2:24 left in the contest, the Buckeyes were perched on the Spartans' 24-yard line. There, with State's Adam's apples swelling, clutch Drake Garrett picked off a pass on his own 11 sealing the victory.

The game was played in a downpour, such that even seeing across the field was a challenge. In part due to the elements, State, which totally dominated the game (running, for example, nearly thirty more offensive plays than the Buckeyes in the first half), could not post a large enough winning margin to prevent falling behind Notre Dame in the national polls.

It was now Purdue and Griese all over again. The Boilermakers were undefeated in the Big Ten, having lost only at Notre Dame in their second game of the campaign. Although a Rose Bowl berth was not at stake for the Spartans, pride, the Big Ten title, and a shot at a national championship were, and that proved more than enough as State pounded Purdue, 41-20. The ever-comical Daugherty explained the looseness of his squad, saying, "We had a little gimmick. One night before practice the coaching staff got together in a huddle and chanted, 'We're #2, we're #2.' I think it took the pressure off." The game was never in question, as State moved out to a 28-0 lead in the third quarter, largely by tormenting Griese with a vicious rush thanks to the efforts of George Webster, Bubba Smith, and company. Raye had a hand in two scores, running in from 17 yards out and throwing for another TD. Bob Apisa added three more touchdowns. Curiously, with 35 points on the board, Duffy still had his first string on the field. "I think what he said was the heck with poor old Jack," said veteran Purdue mentor Jack Mollenkopf, whose team would finish the season 9-2, including a 14-13 win over USC in the Rose Bowl.

The Spartans were now past the critical stage of their schedule. Northwestern, Iowa, and Indiana were all that stood in the path of their second straight Big Ten crown and a season-ending epic confrontation with an almost certain to be undefeated Notre Dame. Even had they combined their squads, the upcoming three Big Ten opponents, whose aggregate mark was 6-22-2 in 1966, hardly seemed capable of beating State. The Spartans registered a shutout in Evanston, as they downed Northwestern 22-0. Clinton Jones and Bob Apisa tallied TDs in the rout, as did Gene Washington on a Jimmy Raye aerial, while Dick Kenney hit on a 39-yard field goal. The Wildcats managed just two first downs and 6 yards rushing in the game.

The Iowa contest resembled a one-sided scrimmage as the Spartans, now in full gear, hammered the Hawkeyes 56-7, after Iowa led 7-0. Duffy would often walk through the locker room before a game and bait his team to be merciless in its attack. The motto with Clinton Jones carrying the pigskin was "Don't Take Any Prisoners." State took none against the hapless Hawkeyes as they generated a breathtaking 607 yards of total offense, 450 on the ground. Clinton Jones ran wild, scoring on TD jaunts of 79, 70, and 29 yards, en route to a then–Big Ten record 268 yards rushing. Jimmy Raye added two touchdown strikes to Gene Washington, one of 53 yards, in the drubbing.

While Notre Dame was devouring Duke 64-0, the Spartans traveled to Indiana and finished off the Hoosiers and another undefeated conference season, 37-19, as Bob Apisa rested his sore knee. Despite the win, the now crotchety Daugherty was unhappy with the squad's pass defense, as the Hoosiers' Frank Stavroff completed twenty-three of his passes for a then–Big Ten record 316 yards. It was a record of near necessity, however, as the green-and-white Goliaths "yielded" –10 yards on thirty-nine rushing attempts. Jimmy Raye provided an offensive highlight, hooking up with Gene Washington on a 64-yard scoring pass.

The Spartans once again dominated conference play. Their 30.4 points per game were even better than 1965 (29.0). Their average of 223.9 yards per game rushing was 32.2 yards better than their nearest competitor, Michigan. Defensively, the Spartans led in points allowed, rushing (just 45.7 with no other league foe under a hundred), and total yardage. Clinton Jones won the rushing title, picking up 593 yards in conference games. State provided four of the conference's top ten scorers. Apisa was 6th with 36 points, followed by punter/placekicker Dick Kenney's 31, and Gene Washington and backup fullback Reggie Cavender's 30. Though making only eighteen receptions, Washington turned five of them into touchdowns and averaged a league-best 22.8 yards per catch. Al Brenner, who pulled in nineteen, was 3rd at 17.3 per reception. Brenner ranked 3rd in punt returns at 15.3. Raye turned in Juday-like passing numbers, ranking 4th in the conference's rating system. In addition to running for 246 yards, Ray hit on 45 of 83 league throws for 847 yards and eight TDs, while being intercepted just three times. His 10.2 yards per attempt easily topped the Big Ten.

Again, it was an all-conference wonderland for the men from East Lansing. Gene Washington, Jerry West, guard Tony Conti, Clinton Jones, and Bob Apisa were among the five Spartans named to either (or both) the AP and UPI first team on offense. Bubba Smith, tackle Nick Jordan, Charles Thornhill, George Webster, and Jesse Phillips in the secondary composed the quintet on the first-team defense. Joe Przbycki and Jimmy Raye were second-team offensive picks, while Phil Hoag, Pat Gallinagh, and tackle Jeff Richardson made it on defense. In sum, fifteen Spartans made either a first or second All–Big Ten squad.

Duffy also was on top of his game. He was riding a fourteen-game conference winning streak, and the back-to-back league titles helped swell his thirteen-year Big Ten record to 52-27-2, with but two losing seasons. His 30-8-1 nonconference and bowl mark helped him to an all-games record of 82-35-3, including ten winning campaigns. Moreover, his teams had scored a whopping 546 points over the past two seasons, yielding just 165, for an average winning margin of more than 19 points. And Duffy's success was not a recent phenomenon, a one- or two-year aberration. Over the past decade he had posted a gaudy 63-26-3 log, turning in eight winning seasons along the way. His Big Ten mark was 42-19-2, with but one losing season.

Duffy and the Spartans were at the summit, but still something was missing: a clear national championship. Furthermore, despite their 9-0 log, the Spartans were ranked #2 nationally, second to the similarly undefeated Fighting Irish. Fortunately, however, the Spartans could rectify that blemish in a week, as well as erase the memory of the

Rose Bowl debacle that marked the first day of the 1966 calendar year, because the game for which legions of football fans nationwide had been waiting all season long was now imminent. Notre Dame would be traveling to East Lansing for a November 19 showdown that would determine who was the nation's best.

CHAPTER 13

Kissing Your Sister

"When you're playing for the national championship, it's not a matter of life and death. It is more important than that."

t seems that each year fans are treated to the most recent "game of the century" in college football, but anyone old enough to remember November 19, 1966, knows there was only such game and it was played at Spartan Stadium. No game since the 1946 Notre Dame–Army encounter in Yankee Stadium, a fierce struggle that ended in a scoreless deadlock, came close to this one in national fervor.

The game simply had everything. Two undefeated teams, ranked #1 and #2, archrivals, putting it all on the line at the end of the season. The game also involved two now truly famous coaches, Duffy Daugherty and Ara Parseghian, both of whom had come within a single game of winning a national championship over the previous two seasons. Duffy had had his chance in 1965. Ara, who had taken over Notre Dame's football hot seat in 1964, had guided the Irish to an almost certain national crown that season, only to be upset in the final game of the campaign by USC.

One of them was almost certain to finish on top in 1966, as Michigan State—ineligible for the Rose Bowl via the no-repeat rule—would play no game after this one, and the Irish, who did not go to postseason bowls as a matter of policy, had only a very beatable Southern Cal team (a squad they would beat 51-0) left on their docket. Moreover, the game crept up on no one. Rather, it was long anticipated to be a classic, so much so that fans began counting down the games on the Michigan State and Notre Dame schedules once it became clear that each university would be fielding a powerhouse in 1966. The week before the game, Daugherty and Parseghian held daily press conferences to assuage a hungry media.

Clearly, these were the best two teams in the land. State had vanquished its foes by an average of 22 points, while the Irish pounded their adversaries by 34. The buildup for the game was simply incredible. Notre Dame's Rocky Bleier recalls in his book, *Fighting Back*, that Michigan State students actually dropped leaflets from an airplane onto the Notre Dame campus. They were addressed to the "peace-loving villagers of Notre Dame," and asked, "Why do you struggle against us? Why do you persist in the mistaken belief that you can win, freely and openly, against us? Your leaders have lied to you. They have led you to believe you can win. They have given you false hope."

Players became truly bigger than life. It was now public knowledge that Charles "Bubba" Smith wore 14D shoes, had a 19½ inch neck, and wore a size 52-long MSU blazer. Smith was the poster child of the confrontation. Referred to as the "intercontinental ballistic Bubba," Spartan coeds wore "Kill, Bubba, Kill" buttons. Smith was so dominant, had become such a legend in his own time, that teams simply ran in the opposite direction from the giant in green and white. Bubba's teammate on the opposite side of the Spartan line, Phil Hoag, actually registered one more tackle for the season (31) than Smith.

Notre Dame received a hazing before they even set foot on the soil of East Lansing. Although there were many fans along the way who cheered for Notre Dame, State fans stood on the railroad platforms in Battle Creek and Kalamazoo as the Irish train, called Grand Trunk, went by. They booed and jeered and held signs proclaiming, "Bubba for Pope," and "Hail Mary, full of grace, Notre Dame's in second place."

The focused Irish did not go to East Lansing to surrender their perch at the top of the polls. This veritable all-star cast of collegians was dealt a near critical blow before ever taking the field, however, as All-American halfback Nick Eddy slipped on the icy train steps. He missed the handrail as he fell and reinjured his tender shoulder. The doubled-over Eddy yelped with pain, fearing that he would not play in the biggest game of his career. He didn't, and the injury sent a shock through the Notre Dame team. The usually jovial bunch was grim as they checked into East Lansing's Jack Tar Hotel under a marquee declaring, "Welcome to the Big One."

It was truly a November football day, cold, overcast, and dreary. The stage could not be better set. Bleier recalls the atmosphere in the stadium. "In the pre-game warmup," he wrote, "I was entranced (almost dizzy, or high!) at the sight of 76,000-plus fans (the official attendance was 80,011) in Spartan Stadium. Nothing I ever experienced on a football field, before or since, has equaled it. The chants rocked and swayed at a deafening level. Try to imagine quadraphonic speakers blasting the Rolling Stones at full volume. It was like that . . . clearly the edge of insanity."

The game began calamitously for the Irish. The Notre Dame center George Goeddeke injured an ankle, courtesy of Smith, on the first series, and the next time the men from the Golden Dome had the ball, a messenger lineman brought in the wrong play—a quarterback draw. The outcome was worse than the Irish faithful could ever have imagined, as their ace sophomore quarterback, Terry Hanratty ran for 4 yards and then into the meat grinder that was George Webster and Bubba Smith. The two behemoths rolled over the signal caller, separating his shoulder.

Beyond the injury, the early going was an ominous sign, particularly for the Irish. The conventional pregame wisdom had it that both teams would shut down the opponent's ground game, leaving the air the only viable option. Given that Notre Dame had enjoyed a strong passing season, this bode reasonably well for the men from South Bend. Hanratty, however, in the brief time he was in the game, attempted four passes, three of which were ludicrously off target.

By Smith's logic, little was gained by the squashing of Hanratty. "That didn't help us any," he said later. "It just let them put in that [Coley] O'Brien who's slippery and faster and gave us more trouble. The other guy just sits there and waits, and that's what we wanted."

The early minutes of the game were marred by myriad miscues. Notre Dame runners were flattened by the likes of Thornhill, Smith, and guard Jeff Richardson. The Irish even muffed a fourth-down punt attempt, owing to a poor snap. Michigan State couldn't cash the coupon, however, fumbling the ball back to Notre Dame. They also managed a delay-of-game infraction, a clip, and another penalty for interfering with the catch of a punt. Amid this football sitcom, however, an opportunity did appear for the Spartans. Gene Washington had beaten the Notre Dame secondary by 10 yards on a broken sprintout pass play. "I can look in a man's eyes and know whether I can beat him," the Big Ten hurdles champion explained. "I knew I could beat those guys all day."

At the close of the first quarter, Raye found Washington for a 42-yard gain. Now near the Notre Dame 30, the Spartans bashed forward with ground attempts before Regis Cavender, in for the injured Bob Apisa, smashed over for a 7-0 advantage.

On their very next possession, the Green and White mounted another drive. Raye ran for 30 yards and then hit Washington for 17 more down to the South Benders 26. Several passes misfired and Dick Kenney hammered a 47-yard field goal through the uprights—10-0 State.

From there, the Notre Dame defense, led by tackle Kevin Hardy and linebackers Jim Lynch and John Horney, stiffened. The Spartans never moved beyond the Irish 47 again. The defense was positively bruising. Spartan ballcarriers were stopped for no gain or tossed for minus yardage no less than sixteen times. The irrepressible Clinton Jones managed but 13 yards in ten carries. Jones took a pounding but delivered one as well. When Lynch snared a second-quarter interception Jones hit him so hard at the knees that the linebacker flipped in the air and landed on his head, fumbling the pigskin back to State in the process and leading to State's field goal.

Just before the half, however, the Irish struck. Hanratty's backup, Coley O'Brien, hit Eddy's backup, Bob Gladieux, for 34 yards and a TD. It was now 10-7. After a dormant third quarter, O'Brien had the Irish on the march. A series of nicely executed runs and passes got the ball down to the State 10. Notre Dame's moving ahead 14-10 seemed imminent, until on third and three O'Brien was trapped by the Spartan defense. Unable to pass, he barely got back to the line of scrimmage. Notre Dame's Joe Azzaro hit on a 28-yard field goal and the game was tied.

This was now truly a game of two halves. The Green and White were clearly superior in the first 30 minutes. Only O'Brien's clutch toss to Gladieux kept the Irish from first-half scoring extinction. In the second half, it was all Notre Dame. Then, with the score knotted at 10, the apparent gamebreaker occurred. Tom Schoen, he of Daugherty's banquet speech mishap, grabbed an off-target Raye aerial and took it 31 yards to the State 18. "Anyone who thought the Irish would pull something besides three straight Larry Conjar plunges and a winning field goal from about the 10- or 15-yard line was in a closed ward somewhere," wrote Dan Jenkins of *Sports Illustrated*.

Although Conjar did carry on first down, the gates to the ward must have been open. The play was followed by Dave Haley going wide, only to have Phil Hoag and Bubba Smith launch him for an eight-yard loss. Parseghian was beside himself later over the blown play. "That Haley play," he moaned, "that was just leakage. We leaked a guy through—blew an assignment." With the ball on the 24, an O'Brien pass failed and it was up to Joe Azzaro once again. This time he narrowly missed from 42 yards out.

Time was now of the essence. Michigan State had been totally squelched in the second half, and Notre Dame had barely missed grabbing the lead. The two heavyweights battled inside the two-minute mark. Then with 1:10 left, Notre Dame took over on its own 30. There was time, but not much time. Then one of the most eerie things happened, something no fan who saw the game live or on television is likely ever to forget. After nearly 59 minutes of slugging it out, Notre Dame quit competing.

The Irish kept the ball on the ground and ran out the clock. Simple and stunning as that. The experience, surreal to the nationwide viewing audience, was completely out of the psychological box for the Spartans. Suddenly it was clear to all. Daugherty, who always played for the win, once said, "A tie is like kissing your sister." Obviously, Parseghian preferred that to embracing more risks. "We couldn't believe it," said George Webster. "When they came up for their first play we kept hollering back and forth, 'Watch the pass, watch the pass.' But they ran. We knew the next one was a pass for sure. But they ran again. We were really stunned. Then it dawned on us. They were settling for tie."

Webster sensed the embarrassment of the Notre Dame squad. "And you know what? They wouldn't even look us in the eyes. They just turned their backs and went back to the huddle," he told the press after the game.

Once the reality of Notre Dame's refusal to compete set in, the State players lost respect for them, staring at the Irish in disdain. Bubba Smith began hollering, "Come on, sissies, throw the ball! I'll call timeout for you." Charley Thornhill joined in, "You don't want it!" Webster was filled with revulsion, shouting, "You're going for the tie, aren't you? You're going for the tie." On the State sidelines, players yelled in anger and helplessness, "Get off the field if you've given up."

O'Brien, a diabetic, necessitating two insulin shots a day, was exhausted. He drank orange juice and consumed candy bars on the sidelines to maintain his insulin level. He was so wired that he could recall little or none of the action. Notre Dame was concerned that he was now so spent that to air it out in the last minute could have a disastrous effect, one of throwing the game to the Green and White wolves, or at least so the story goes. "We'd fought hard to come back and tie it up," said Parseghian to a disbelieving press. "After all that, I didn't want to risk giving it to them cheap. They get reckless and it could have cost them the game. I wasn't going to do a stupid thing like that."

There were indeed two points of view. In the Irish locker room Parseghian was emotional. "Men, I'm proud of you," he said. "God knows I've never been more proud of any group of young men in my life. Get one thing straight, though. We did not lose. We were #1 when we came; we fell behind, had some tough things happen, but overcame them. No one could have wanted to win this one more than I. We didn't win, but we did not lose. They're crying about a tie, trying to detract from your efforts. They're trying to make it come out a win. Well, you don't believe it. Their season is over. They can't go anywhere. It's all over and we're still #1. Time will prove everything that has happened here today. And you'll see that after the rabble-rousers have had they say, cooler minds who understand the true odds will know that Notre Dame is a team of champions."

From the other side, the issue was integrity and honor. Notre Dame had, in a word, stopped competing. The Fighting Irish had all but said, "We know you, State, will probably beat us if we keep playing, so we will freeze this game down to one of fifty-eight minutes and fifty seconds, rather than sixty minutes." They would quit on the field and win the national championship at the polls. For millions there was something rankly dishonorable about that. Certainly that was the case for Daugherty—though he was gracious enough not to go public about it—a coach who never, ever went for the tie no matter the situation, one who lobbied intensely for an overtime system that would prevent any and all deadlocks.

For many, Parseghian's argument was not sufficiently compelling. Surely he could have employed a trick play—a reverse, a flea flicker, a halfback option—something to get the ball to, say, midfield, call time out and then try to move into Azzaro's range. Even if he did fail, there would have been honor in that. Perhaps the freshness of losing a national championship in the last 1:33 of a season-ending game against USC just two years previous constrained Parseghian to drain the clock. Whatever the reason, he never budged off his decision.

According to Collegefootballnews.com's excellent summation, "In the history of college football, there might not have been a game with more of a feeling of emptiness and dissatisfaction than this one. If a tie is like kissing your sister, this chick looked like Beano Cook." The publication did not accept the excuse of O'Brien's diabetic exhaustion, suggesting, "They could've found an apple for him to eat." And more was lost than tied for the men from South Bend. "In the eyes of football fans," the report went on, "the disappointment turned into contempt for the Irish for playing it so safe when Michigan State pulled out all the stops to try and win the game."

Despite Alabama's going undefeated, the pollsters came through for Parseghian. Both the AP and UPI crowned the Irish national champions. State was second in both polls (losing 506-471 on voting points in the AP, and by just five—329-324—in the UPI).

Duffy was very unhappy with the pollsters, who kept Notre Dame on top of the national gridiron heap. Despite the second-half brownout, the Spartans outrushed, outpassed, and gained more first downs than the Irish in the 10-10 deadlock. "We dominated that game in every department," he said year later, "and to this day I don't understand why AP rated Notre Dame #1. The Irish went out and walloped Southern California badly at the tail end of the year, so perhaps that influenced some voters."

State hardly dominated, as the box score suggests.

	MSU	ND
First Downs	3	10
Rush Yardage	142	91
Pass Yardage	142	128
Passes	7-20	8-25
Had Intercepted	3	1
Punts	8-38	8-42
Fumbles Lost	1	1
Yards Penalized	32	5

For Michigan State, Raye was the hero and the villain. He ran twenty-one times for 75 yards, by far the best mark for either team. Regrettably for the junior quarterback, the position also mandated that he throw, and that he did poorly, hitting on just seven of twenty attempts and being picked three times.

The two-year magic carpet ride was now over. And what a ride it had been: a 19-1-1 record with the Spartans scoring 556 points and yielding but 175. The 381-point spread tapped out to an average winning margin of better than 18 points an outing. Moreover, the team had outscored its conference opposition 416-127 as it ran off fourteen straight Big Ten wins.

With Jones, Washington, Webster, and Smith, all black players, now off to the NFL as marquee names among its rookies—Smith and Jones went one-two, while all four were selected in the top ten—the fifty-one-year-old Daugherty had some holes to patch for 1967.

CHAPTER 14

The Year After

"That kid has a four-year scholarship. My contract is a one-year deal. Let him make his own decisions."

—Duffy's response to an occasion in which he left the decision on a critical play to his quarterback

"The era of the fantastic athlete at Michigan State is over," Daugherty declared at the outset of the 1967 campaign. "We had a windfall of exceptional individual stars that made us an outstanding team for two years. Now they're gone and we're back to playing the boys again."

In addition to the big four, Duffy lost fourteen other seniors off the 1966 powerhouse. The sting figured to be felt particularly on defense. Gone were seven of the top ten tacklers from the 1966 squad that ranked 3rd in the nation in rushing defense. Worse, Jesse Phillips had developed a nasty habit of writing check overdrafts. With Phillips out, the secondary yielded a ghastly 323 yards though the air in the spring game, an ominous sign.

Sports Illustrated, though declaring State as the preseason Big Ten favorite (and therefore likely the first team in league history to notch three straight championships), noted the change in the Green and White profile. "The students no longer gather at

115

the feet of the bronze statue of Sparty, which commands the tricornered intersection outside Michigan State football stadium, shouting slogans like 'Kill, Bubba, Kill!' and 'Crush the Irish,'" it noted. "Instead they are measuring Sparty for an olive branch." It was enough to make a grown man like Duffy Daugherty cry, the publication asserted, a man who had bred "more prize studs for the pros than Calumet Farm."

Offensively things looked better. Although Jones was gone, the next ten rushers were back. Bob Apisa had had off-season knee surgery and missed spring practice, but the now-married fullback had no peer when healthy. Apisa sounded confident when he said, "I want to play, and I know the leg will be all right." Backup fullback Regis Cavender, 200-pound human sledgehammer Dwight Lee, and sophomore LaMarr Thomas could also be counted upon. Then there was Jimmy Raye, who could both run and throw and was now touted by many as Juday's superior. Although Washington had departed, speedy Al Brenner, who caught twenty-two tosses the previous season, was back for Raye to use as his target.

Although admitting "it's the defense that will make or break us," the ever-optimistic Daugherty counted on the likes of Raye, Brenner, and co-captains Drake Garrett and offensive lineman Tony Conti to form the nucleus of another contender in 1967. The key to the schedule figured to be games four through eight, when the Green and White would face Michigan, Minnesota, Notre Dame, and Ohio State in back-to-back tests, the first three of which would be on the road.

A throng of 75,833 piled into Spartan Stadium for the opener against what figured to be the first victim of the 1967 Spartans, the team from the University of Houston. Daugherty had agreed to play the Cougars as a favor to his former assistant Bill Yeoman, who was now the Houston head mentor. Duffy was feeling good, particularly about his Raye-led offense. "We expect Jimmy Raye to be a more mature, consistent quarterback," he stated on the day before the game. "Anyone who doesn't respect his throwing might get surprised. We've got some fine runners, and I've never been so confident that a Michigan State team would go out there tomorrow and do a good job."

Houston had already defeated Florida State in the opener, and as Duffy said, "It's an old saying but a true one that a college team improves more between its first and second games than it does all year." Nonetheless, the Spartans figured to prevail. "We'll make some first game errors," Duffy added, "but I hope we'll be good enough to overcome them."

To stay loose, a number of the Cougar players claimed the game was really for the Beaumont, Texas, city championship. Amazingly, this town of approximately 120,000 in northeast Texas had supplied eight players for this contest, four on each team, one of whom was State's Tody Smith, Bubba's brother.

State had swagger. At the stadium before Houston arrived on Friday, the Spartans dressed first, crowded into the tunnel outside the Houston locker room, and began their intimidation ritual of shouts, chants, growls, clapping, and cleat-stomping. Yeoman, familiar with the routine, assured his squad, "They can holler in the tunnel, but you play football out on that field."

A day later, with the pregame psychological warfare concluded, the Spartans took the field against the visitors. The good news is that the game was a blowout. The bad news is that Houston won.

As it turned out it was not Jimmy Raye, but lightning fast scatback Warren McVea (of Beaumont), who was all the rage on this 23rd of September. The first time "Mac the Knife" touched the ball he jaunted 48 yards. The second time it was 33. Weaving this way and that, all over the field, veteran State tacklers like Jesse Phillips and Drake Garrett were in awe. "He's the best back I've ever seen," said Garrett, who had seen Clinton Jones tear up the gridiron for the Green and White. "His moves . . . you don't know what he'll do next . . . he's there . . . and then he's not."

When McVea was not dazzling the Spartan defense on the ground, quarterback Dick Woodall was owning the airways. Operating from a pro-style spread formation, he hit Kenny Hebert and Don Bean on touchdown-scoring bombs. Raye was less successful. The State signal caller was picked off by Mike Simpson, who took the interception in from 41 yards out.

The final score was 37-7.

McVea was jubilant. He wondered aloud if his Beaumont buddy Smith would be waiting for him after the game. "I want to talk to him about the killin'," he told the press. As for Duffy, there was comfort that four other of the nation's top ten teams lost on this day—Miami, Alabama, Arkansas, and Texas. A bit in shock, the fifty-two-year-old mentor remained upbeat while crediting Yeoman's squad, one that would go 7-3 for the season. "We're not this bad," he assured his listeners, "but even if we'd played better, it only would have made the score closer. That team of theirs, you either catch 'em for a loss, or boom!"

In game two, State drew the team that would finish the 1967 season #1 in the nation, the USC Trojans. It was a thriller for the East Lansing faithful. Although quarterback Steve Sogge spread the Spartan secondary, hitting on fourteen of his sixteen mostly short passing attempts, and Heisman Trophy winner O.J. Simpson rumbled for 190 yards on a whopping thirty-six carries, the Spartans trailed just 21-17 late in the game, after actually leading 17-14 at the half. The more than 75,000 fans then watched their favorites drive some 75 yards down to the Southern Cal five. There the Spartans faked an option and hurled a TD strike to clutch Al Brenner for what would have been the winning score. It wasn't —as an official flagged the play, claiming the other State end had been blocking downfield. Later films indicated the referee had been incorrect.

Winless Wisconsin could not have appeared at a better time for Daugherty's beleaguered charges. With Dwight Lee and LaMarr Thomas leading the way, State ran over the hapless Badgers, 35-7.

The respite was brief, however, as the Green and White headed to Ann Arbor, where the Wolverines prepared to get even with Duffy's team, having lost the last two confrontations by a combined 44-14. Slumping Jimmy Raye was concerned during the week before the game at Michigan. "I had felt the weight of the world was on my shoulders," said the quarterback about life before the Michigan game. "I felt people were saying, 'Jimmy Raye, you are a bum.'" To ready himself, Raye studied some 1966 films and put in extra practice with assistant Al Dorow. It paid off. The savvy senior accounted for four TDs, two on the ground and another pair in the air. He had been wired all week. "But I was relaxed today," he said after the game. "I decided to just have fun." The whole team had fun, defeating their despised rivals by an almost unbelievable 34-0 margin.

Now 2-0 in the Big Ten, the Spartans were tied with Purdue for the top spot in the league. A strong Minnesota team in Minneapolis was next. Duffy was just 2-5 against the Gophers over the years, one of just two Big Ten teams (Iowa was the other) against which Daugherty was under .500 during his first thirteen seasons. Coach Murray Warmath, under the gun in Minnesota after fielding some strong squads earlier in the decade, risked greater fan displeasure by starting the previous season's good-run, weak-pass Curt Wilson at quarterback. Warmath, hoping to loosen State's defense a tad with some early passes to set up the run, watched Wilson hurl fourteen completions in twenty-five attempts for 262 yards and three touchdowns. After having yielded only 7 points in its last two outings—scoring 69—the Spartans were shut out 21-0.

It was time to flush the Gopher game away, because the rematch with Notre Dame had now arrived. This one, however, would be in South Bend. The Irish were beatable, having lost twice already in part due to a soft ground game. Duffy had no time for sympathy. He had troubles of his own. Not only had his team lost thrice, but

Jimmy Raye was out with bruised ribs and the coach had suspended six players for violating curfew. Expecting Notre Dame to rely on Terry Hanratty's arm, Parseghian surprised the State defenders by sending fullback Jeff Zimmerman through the line for 135 yards and two TDs. Hanratty hit Zimmerman for a third score en route to an easy 24-12 conquest of the Spartans.

Michigan State was now in a free fall, and Daugherty was helpless to stop it, not with powerful Ohio State, surprising Indiana, and consistently tough Purdue ahead.

The Buckeyes were first, defeating State easily by a 21-7 margin in East Lansing. What was particularly disheartening for Daugherty was that Woody Hayes's ground chuck offense had managed to have its quarterback, Bill Long, complete nine of his eleven passes. Not that Woody abandoned the overland route; he sent fullback Paul Huff crashing into the Spartan defense for 120 yards and two touchdowns. Now 2-5, Duffy was philosophical. "I guess it's as easy to get used to losing as it is to winning," he said disingenuously.

Indiana was the story of the Big Ten for 1967. Perennial bottom-feeders (the Hoosiers were a toxic 14-50-1 over the previous seven seasons), Indiana was 7-0. With four of its seven wins by 5 points or less, the oddsmakers weren't buying, as they installed the Spartans as favorites in part because the game would be played at Spartan Stadium. Nonetheless, it had been a year to remember in the Hoosier state. "God is not dead." the quip went. "He plays right end for Indiana in the fourth quarter."

Not surprisingly, Indiana trailed 13-7 in the game's closing minutes. Also not surprisingly, the Hoosiers then put together a last-gasp drive, with halfback John Isenbarger picking up 52 yards on the march before entering the promised land from seven yards out for the winning score in a 14-13 victory. Although the Hoosiers had been "a laugh-a-minute" team, with "error-prone sophomore backs and Katzenjammer Kids defense," they did not take well to being underdogs to an already five-loss team. "That," said Coach John Pont, "was an incentive for us. It irritated everybody."

The dispirited Spartans fell at Purdue 21-7 the next week, stretching their losing skein to five, with only a home date with 3-6 Northwestern left on the docket. The season had now become a nightmare for the 2-7 State (2-5 in the conference), and the fans had had it. Only 45,022 showed up to watch the Spartans roll to a 42-27 win over the Wildcats.

Were it not for Illinois, the 3-4 Spartans would have come in last in the Big Ten in total offensive yardage. They were 8th on defense. No Spartan made the top ten in rushing, passing, pass receiving, or total offense. Only tackle Joe Przybycki made

All–Big Ten (second team) on offense, while end George Chatlos, a first-team pick, was the only defensive honoree.

Eternal optimist that he continued to be, Duffy had foreseen more happy times for the Spartans in 1967, only to experience the humiliation of defeat. After the season he would tell his audiences, "We won three, lost none and were upset seven times."

CHAPTER 15

Green, White, and Black

**"A good coach never asks one of his assistants to do something he
wouldn't do himself, so I saved [recruiting in] the Hawaii territory for
myself."**

The 1968 season opened at home against a so-so Syracuse squad in East Lansing.
With State down 10-7 in the final period, the Spartans had the ball on the Orangemen eight. Quarterback Bill Feraco went back to throw and slipped. Just as
disaster seemed certain, Feraco righted himself, made it past the Syracuse pass rushers and crossed the goal for a 14-10 Green and White victory. A weak Baylor was next
and the Spartans took advantage. Feraco hit Al Brenner six times in a nine-of-thirteen
passing day and State was 2-0 after a 28-10 triumph. Things were really looking up
when State visited feckless Wisconsin, trampling the Badgers 39-0 in Camp Randall.

With the Detroit Tigers grabbing the sports headlines in the World Series, 102,785
fans crowded into the Ann Arbor Big House for the Wolverines' date with State. Curiously, Daugherty and Elliot shared the same television coach's show originating out of
Detroit. Daugherty, who almost certainly outshone the staid Chalmers "Bump" Elliot

with the pancake makeup applied, hoped his charges would outshine Michigan on the field as well.

They almost did, leading 14-13 in the final quarter. It was not to be, however, as the stronger Wolverines emerged with a 28-14 triumph. The key play turned out to be one in which the mobile Michigan quarterback, Dennis Brown, was almost flattened by a tidal wave of sack-hungry Spartans at midfield, only to have the wily signal caller lob a pass to team ace Jim Mandich at the twenty-five, who took it in from there.

Still 3-1, the Spartans welcomed Minnesota into Spartan Stadium a week later. Spartan fans, expecting a solid win against the Gophers, were dismayed when their heroes trailed 14-7 late in the game. The skies brightened, however, when sophomore quarterback Bill Triplett hit end Frank Foreman for a 17-yard TD. Duffy was no Ara. He detested "kissing his sister." With Spartan Stadium rocking, the Green and White went for the two-point conversion and the win, but the play broke down and the inexplicable Minnesota hex continued. The Gophers had now won seven of the last nine meetings.

The reeling Spartans were now looking down the barrel at #5 Notre Dame. The night before the game, Daugherty held court and had everybody laughing, as he told legendary ND Athletic Director Moose Krause that he might just open the contest with an onside kick. "But nobody takes me seriously," cracked a grinning Daugherty.

Notre Dame should have, as the Spartans covered a game-opening onside kick on the Irish 42. Shortly later, Tommy Love raced in from 11 yards out and Spartan fans began hoping for an upset. Senior Notre Dame T-man Terry Hanratty was clutch, however, hitting on twenty-seven of forty-three passes for 312 yards, in addition to running for 43 more. Nonetheless, the Green and White defense, led by safety (and split end) Al Brenner, permitted just 17 points and MSU, with the help of another Love TD, defeated mighty Notre Dame, 21-17.

The victory over Notre Dame gave the men from East Lansing a 4-2 mark and a date in Columbus against #2 Ohio State. Even that ranking was too low, for the undefeated Buckeyes were probably the nation's best. There was action even before the game. Woody Hayes, realizing that Daugherty was always looking for the psychological edge, noticed the genial mentor talking with one of Woody's defensive stars, Jim Stillwagon. "How're you?" Daugherty asked with seeming innocence.

"What are you doing here?" Woody demanded of Daugherty. Before Duffy could respond, the near paranoid coach turned to Stillwagon and ordered, "Don't listen to this guy! He's just trying to soften you up." Then back to Daugherty: "You get back up on that field or I'm going to kick your butt."

There was plenty of butt kicking in the contest. Woody, concerned about Daugherty's ingenuity and fearing an upset at the hands of the sly Spartan mentor, decided to employ some ingenuity of his own. The usual grind-it-out coach ordered passing plays even on first down. And if that were not enough, Hayes used a no-huddle offense. The Buckeyes scored the first two TDs and led 13-0 in the second quarter before MSU quarterback Bill Triplett smashed over from the one to draw within six. Powerful Buckeye Jim Otis powered over for his second score before the half, and the teams went into the intermission with Ohio State up by a 19-7 count.

Things became very interesting in the third quarter when the Spartans' Triplett hit Frank Foreman for a 13-yard TD, turning the game into a 19-14 contest. A two-yard plunge by backup quarterback Ron Maciejowski (in for injured star Rex Kern) pushed the margin to a safer 25-14. But Duffy's troops had stamina, and when Tommy Love hit pay dirt from a yard out, the 84,859 fans had reason for anxiety. A two-point conversion would pull MSU within a field goal. The conversion attempt—a pass—failed, however, and the score was 25-20 with still a quarter remaining.

MSU had the ball when Ohio State delivered the clincher. With Triplett back to throw, defensive end Mark Debevec came crashing through, smashing into the Spartan T-man and forcing a fumble in the process. Debevec's counterpart on the other side of the Buckeye defensive line, Dave Whitfield, covered the bobble and Ohio State's undefeated season and Rose Bowl destiny was secured.

For the Spartans it was a blown game. They turned it over an unforgivable seven times—three interceptions and four fumbles. "Once again, we beat ourselves," said a disconsolate Daugherty. "You can't turn the ball over that often. When you turn the ball over seven times to a team as good as Ohio State, it's a wonder if you don't get beat worse than that." In the fourth quarter, the Buckeyes really played with a sense of urgency, flattening Spartan ballcarriers for losses six times.

Despite being outgained 429-271, MSU had a shot at victory. Three times late in the contest MSU had a drive aborted on bizarre plays resulting in fumbles. "We had no one to blame but ourselves for that loss," acknowledged the coach mournfully, "but when you blow a chance to knock off the #1 team it hurts more than ever."

The Ohio State battle was followed by a home contest against a beatable Hoosier team in East Lansing. Duffy created a legion of Monday-morning quarterbacks in what turned out to be as grinding a 24-22 loss as any coach could imagine. On fourth and one near the Indiana goal, Daugherty rejected a fourth-quarter field goal, opting to go for six. It was the wrong decision. Then, in the final minute, the Spartans were driving again, with a first and goal at the Indiana one. The automatic field goal would give the Spartans 25 points, all but placing them out of reach of the spirited Hoosiers.

The snap was fumbled along with the game, as Indiana scored with 22 seconds left. The following Monday at the barbershop, unbeknownst to a group of fans who were simply roasting the coach, the man sitting in the chair with his back to the gathering was none other than Duffy. The venting was fierce. "Stupid Duffy" . . . "Can't the idiot add?" . . . "The dummy blew it" . . . "Doesn't that clown realize . . . ?" Finally the barber, entertained by the goings on, asked when the guys had figured out what Daugherty should have done.

One customer had thought of it Saturday evening while downing a few beers, another when watching "smart" pro coaches the following day. With that, Duffy turned in his chair, faced his critics, and delivered a verbal shot. "I realized what I should have done even before I got back to the locker room on Saturday afternoon. What took you so long?"

The once-promising season was slipping away for State. The slip became a three-game slide the following week as the Spartans fell 9-0 in a fumble-driven defeat to a powerful Purdue squad at Spartan Stadium. Bumbling defeats are particularly upsetting to any coach, and Duffy was no exception. Once in a turnover-ridden defeat at Purdue, there was a bit of comic relief amid the pain. As the Spartans were making their way to their dressing after a sloppy first half, the State drum major uncharacteristically dropped his baton after tossing it in the air over the goalposts. The item bounced crazily and embarrassingly about the end zone, leaving one leather lung to holler, "Is Duffy coaching the band, too?"

Amid the humor, there was tension. Duffy had been the first coach ever to recruit black players out of the South. He claimed no great nobility for having done so, maintaining that he recruited these African American young men because they were good football players. He did insist, however, that there never was a real issue among black athletes at State, although there was plenty of ferment within the university at large, as was the case throughout the nation.

This was the 1960s, and by April 4, 1968, racial unrest had gone from simmer to boil on the national front. On that night Martin Luther King Jr. was assassinated in Memphis. John Matthew Smith ("Breaking the Pane") recounts a speech given by

Michigan State educational psychology professor Robert L. Green—a colleague of King's in the Southern Christian Leadership Conference—in the wake of shooting. Green pointed out that, despite the signal contributions of black athletes to the prestige of the university, there was not a single African American coach in the athletic department. Two weeks later, President Hannah and Athletic Director Clarence "Biggie" Munn hired former star Don Coleman as a football assistant, a move that smacked of tokenism to black players.

Spokesman LaMarr Thomas confronted Munn with a list of grievances, demanding Munn sign a document assuring them he would take the bill of particulars to Hannah. When, according to Thomas, Munn refused, a boycott ensued. It hit the football program in the solar plexus, as two dozen players walked out of the spring practice on April 25.

There were few things for which Daugherty was less prepared than this. Empowered by the Black Student Association and the Black Power ethic of the era, the players wanted more than just black coaches. They wanted African American cheerleaders, administrative staff, and other workers. The players, with their scholarships at risk, were addressing systematic racism at the institutional level.

For Duffy, this had to be perplexing. He had always made race an individual thing—a personal element—trying to be fair and hospitable. How could this be happening? He was on the defensive in a way he had never imagined. After all, wasn't he the first coach to recruit black players from the South? And didn't they realize he did so, not because they were black, but because they were solid football players?

Daugherty betrayed his naïveté in referring to the revolt as the "black problem," all the while dissociating it from football. Referring dismissively to the Black Student Association as the Black Student Alliance, "There was a problem on campus as there was all across the country but it had nothing whatsoever to do with football," Duffy stated in his autobiography. Being a football coach, not a sociologist, there was an understandable disconnect in his thinking. He could not link the local concerns of his black players to the national drama of institutional racism. The situation in the Spartan locker room was microcosm of a nationwide toxin, but that was beyond Daugherty's line of vision.

In fairness to Daugherty, the bringing in of Coleman was a significant act, even if in response to outside pressure. The presence of African Americans on major college football staffs is of no great moment today; however, it is safe to say that very, very few programs had even a single black person in even an assistant's role in the 1960s. Of note is that Daugherty was not the least bit threatened by the activism of the Black Student Association. Though lacking a sophisticated knowledge of institutional discrimination, he had developed sufficiently authentic relationships with his African American players such that he was not overly concerned about being one of their targets.

In that era, many cross-racial alliances were of an official, ritualized nature, such that white bureaucrats, aware that they knew not a single black person personally, lived in fear of confrontation and particularly of being labeled as racist. There simply was so little substance, so little traction in most of these student-administrator relationships, let alone student-faculty associations. What existed was a silent tension, one that might break open at any point and over any incident, and such an eruption would leave those whites in power immobilized because they simply had no prior experience with issues having a racial edge. Again, Daugherty had over a decade of personal experience relating to black players and their families and, confident of the quality of those relationships, he was able to move through the immediate crisis with his respect intact.

Nonetheless, with the boycott under way, the coach was backed into a corner. He did have some nonnegotiable rules, one of which was that no player was allotted more than two unexcused absences. The third would spell the end of his tenure on the team. The players, not wanting to be dropped from the squad but wanting to stand for solidarity, asked Daugherty if he would suspend the rule for the moment. He refused.

The players missed a practice. Astutely, Daugherty made no public announcement on the matter. Tensions were rising all around. Then President Hannah came to the rescue. He first asked Daugherty if he would excuse the African American athletes from the next workout. Duffy didn't like it, feeling it would undermine team unity. Hannah wanted the black players to meet with Dr. John Fuzak, the faculty athletic representative, believing some resolution might be reached there. Daugherty wisely agreed to a compromise. He called off practice for the entire team while the meeting was held. The issues were raised, a settlement was reached, and football resumed.

That Daugherty was uncompromising concerning the rules is interesting in retrospect. Here a case might be made that although he had some understanding of the importance of the concerns of his athletes, he perhaps did not appreciate them sufficiently. Giving them a waiver on an additional workout or two would hardly seem too soft, given the incredibly volatile temper of the moment. Here again one could question Daugherty's depth of understanding of the intensity of the racial ferment of the times. It is striking, however, that his players, though wishing he might cut a few yards of additional slack, did not turn on him. Clearly they saw him as, at best, an ally, and, at worst, not one of the barriers to their future as emerging African American adults in a now racially aware society.

In any case, Daugherty was very sensitive about the publicity surrounding the incident. He was very pleased about his relationships with all his athletes, particularly the racial tone on his team, and expended considerable energy informing the public that the issues at State were not about the nature of the football program, as indicated in his autobiography. There was, however, another small flap. It involved Bubba Smith through his brother, Tody, who left the university to play at USC.

The Smiths were from Beaumont, Texas, where Bubba and Tody's father was a very successful high school football coach. In fact, Daugherty had attempted to recruit Bubba's older brother, Willie Ray, before him, but the youngster went to Iowa, was unhappy, and left. According to Duffy, the elder Smith called Duffy about Bubba, hoping that State would take a chance on him and "try to make a man out of him."

Duffy begged off initially, telling Coach Smith that if his own father couldn't effect the desired maturity, it was unlikely that Duffy would succeed in the effort. Smith persisted and Duffy relented, not without realizing how incredibly talented Bubba was. Bubba Smith was not very coachable. He did not hustle. Burt Smith, the new athletic director, could not spark anything. Neither could defensive line coach Hank Bullough. When Bullough essentially gave up, Daugherty offered only one solution: "Put him on the scouting team and forget about him."

That seemed to do it. Smith came to Duffy's office, wanting to know why he had been written off. Duffy was ready with the challenge. "Bubba, you're either going to be a great All-American for Michigan State, or you're not going to play a single minute of varsity football" is how Daugherty remembers phrasing it. "It's as simple as that. You refuse to go all out, and if you don't give a hundred percent, you don't play for me."

Smith reminded the coach that he was better than anyone else on the field.

Daugherty gave him no argument, other than to remind him that talent unused was talent wasted. He went on to suggest to Bubba that if he didn't want to stay at MSU, the coach would see if anyone else might want to take a chance on him. Smith would have none of it and opted to go all out. In the scrimmage that followed Smith became so enraged when two of the first-teamers drove him back and onto the ground in a two-on-one situation that he kicked one of them in the head.

Daugherty lost it and went after Smith physically. Smith, who could have destroyed the portly coach with one mighty motion, was perhaps more stunned than anything else. In any case, Daugherty sent him to the sidelines, telling him there was simply no place in the game for someone who acted as he did. Shortly later Smith headed into the locker room. When the coach came in after practice, Smith asked for a final opportunity. Several days later, one of the offensive linemen was neutralizing Smith consistently. Bullough began getting on Bubba, asking why he wasn't breaking through the offensive line. "The offensive man is holding me," he said, "but I'm afraid to belt him because of what the man over there [Daugherty] might do."

The coaches resolved the matter, and of course Smith became a literal legend in Michigan State football lore. Although Smith now bought into the team concept, he would continue to test Duffy. Once when Smith had a shiny new car, two problems arose. The first was the appearance of impropriety raised by the very existence of the vehicle. Some thought a booster had given it to the now famous senior. Duffy thought it may have been an NFL team. Smith insisted his father had obtained a bank loan for it. Smith proved honorable, as Duffy checked with Bubba's father and the bank. The second problem was that Smith decided to defy a team rule and park the obvious vehicle right outside the stadium where players were forbidden to park cars.

"Charles Smith," Duffy said sternly, ready to engage in some brinkmanship, "you have precisely five minutes to get that car out of there, or you can get in it and drive straight back to Beaumont."

Although Smith moved the car and continued a path of gridiron greatness, his was a strange relationship with Daugherty, according to the coach's autobiography. Smith would vacillate between euphoric behavior and sulking, between open shows of affection for Daugherty and unbridled criticism. When things were not going well for Tody, Bubba became publicly critical of his handling by Duffy and the staff. Yet when Daugherty was in California on a television assignment after his retirement from coaching, a large pair of brown hands suddenly encapsulated his neck. It was the affectionate Bubba. "Coach, I don't know how you ever put up with me," he said.

Daugherty had no answer, because he also wondered how he had endured. He was, however, very glad he did.

In contrast to his public image as comedian and entertainer, Duffy was a man of considerable depth, one who had thought through the role of coach in its most profound sense.

The 4-5 Spartans, with still a chance at a .500 season, packed their bags for Evanston, Illinois, and a date with Northwestern. The trip proved successful, as State rolled over the Wildcats 31-14, with Triplett running for three TDs and throwing for a fourth.

The 5-5 log was a disappointment. The home losses to Minnesota and Indiana (who were a combined 10-8 outside of their games with MSU) were particularly galling. Those two defeats spelled the difference between a healthy 7-3 season and a mediocre .500 campaign. Toss in the giveaway losses to Ohio State and Purdue and the Spartans were that close to a 9-1 resurgence. The four defeats were by a combined 17 points. To paraphrase Bill Parcells, however, you are what your record says you are. Don't tell me you're just 17 points from being 9-1. All you're telling me is that you can't win the close ones. Michigan State was a 5-5 team in 1968.

Despite their sorry 2-5 conference record, the Spartans proved tough on defense, finishing 2nd in total yards, yielding but 293.7 per contest. They were also runners-up in rushing defense at 155.1 per outing. Unfortunately, they lost the turnover battle by just under one a game. Tom Love's 461 rushing yards placed 8th in the league, while Bill Triplett ranked 8th in passing and total offense. Dick Berlinski led in punting yards per attempt (39.3), while Frank Waters's four interceptions tied him for 4th in the Big Ten.

CHAPTER 16

Surviving

"I didn't penalize him for backfield in motion. I penalized the other ten guys on your team for delay of game."

—A Duffy favorite about a coach complaining to an official over repeated false start calls

The times, they were a changing. And you could see it. In 1969 Spartan Stadium installed artificial turf.

The ever-ingenious Duffy was tired of mediocrity. He needed to do something to jump-start his offense, so he went to the triple option. The point of the offensive system is to move beyond the defensive tackle and end without having to block them. "That was easy for us," cracked Duffy, "we never blocked them anyhow."

Daugherty would need something because the schedule was homicidal. The Spartans faced every conference contender—#1 (preseason) Ohio State, #11 Indiana, and #12 Purdue. In addition, they faced the #8 Irish and #17 SMU out of the Big Ten.

Fortunately, the season opened at home against a Washington Husky team that would win but one game in 1969. It would not come at State, as Duffy's charges defeated the team from the state of apples, 27-11. A real test figured to follow. Southern

Methodist was coming in with focus. Ranked #17 in the preseason, the Mustangs had lost their first two games. They left 0-3, as the Green and White prevailed 23-15.

Notre Dame was waiting in South Bend, bent on avenging the 21-17 loss of the previous season. With quarterback Joe Theismann connecting on twenty of thirty-three passing attempts for 294 yards, the Irish won by two touchdowns, 28-14. The upending at South Bend was followed by a second straight trip to Columbus. This proved no repeat of the 25-20 squeaker a season ago. The potent Buckeyes mauled Daugherty's team by a whopping 54-21 margin. The 54-point explosion was humiliating for Daugherty. No previous opponent had ever scored as many as 40 against one of his teams.

Duffy was now under fire. He had gone just 8-12 in the previous two campaigns and was now a lackluster 2-2. Worse, he had been pounded by a combined 96-49 in his last two outings. Worse still, Michigan was coming in next, a team that would be in the Rose Bowl in January 1970.

The game would be the first against Michigan State for new Wolverine coach Bo Schembechler, who studied the films and readied his team to shut down the staggering State team. Duffy, however, was down but not out. Overmatched and facing nearly certain defeat, Daugherty decided to surprise Michigan with a completely different look. He scrapped the triple option, although his squad had averaged 24.8 points per game in its first four contests, and went back to the Power I set.

Duffy took the young Bo to school. He began by telling the media that he would try an onside kick if the opportunity presented itself early in the game, and he did just that en route to a rousing 23-12 upset of a Rose Bowl–bound Michigan squad. But to Bo and everyone else's surprise, Daugherty's strategic wizardry was not confined to a single play.

"He really fooled us," recalled Michigan's Schembechler. "He was running the wishbone and all week long we practiced against the wishbone. So, on Saturday, he runs the I-formation and we didn't know what we were doing and were confused all day long. Duffy put one over on us."

The jolly Irishman was full of quips after this caper. "I've got a good chance to be in Pasadena," he told the press, "because I can buy a plane ticket. I don't know about my football team."

Schembechler came to have great affection for Daugherty. "I liked Duffy a lot," he said. "I was going to one of his clinics in Boston and was sitting in the back of the plane. Duffy, of course, was up front. After we took off, he came back to see me. He was mad. He said, 'We can't have you sitting back here.' He walked away in a huff, and five minutes later I was sitting with him in first class."

The Bo-Duffy bond endured beyond Daugherty's coaching days, and Schembechler's regard for Daugherty says much about the esteem in which Duffy was held by his highly regarded colleagues. "He was something else," Bo recalled. "He would call me every year. He never missed, and he would give me a big play over the telephone. He'd say, 'Get a pencil and pad. Write it down. This one is great, Bo. It can't miss. Write it down just as I tell you and you'll surprise the heck out of them.' Every year, a different call, a different play. You had to love the guy."

Coaching was teaching for Duffy Daugherty, and it began with player relations, a particular strength of Daugherty's. Beyond being a technician, a coach "must be a student of human relations, an educator of outstanding insight and perception of the interactions of people," he said in *1st and Ten*. He did not take himself too seriously, had an empathic streak, and did not focus on myriad rules. "The coach, by arbitrary techniques, can cause the members of his particular team to react and behave in clear-cut, stereotyped patterns," he noted.

For Daugherty, discipline had little to do with hair length or formal behavior in an era in which authority figures imposed just such external limits on young people as a way of maintaining control, if only symbolically. This was especially true as it related to black athletes. Many coaches objected to large Afros—virtually the fashion norm of the times, and to goatees and mustaches, very nearly a cultural staple of manhood among African Americans—simply because they were uneasy about how these surface expressions clashed with the conservative styles with which they were comfortable. For many less-aware coaches, bushy Afros, beards, and goatees made statements of individual or racial identity, statements that separated the black athletes from the homogenized look these mentors preferred. These looks were perceived as acts of defiance or at least nonconformity, anathema to many head coaches with a paramilitary mien.

Moreover, when conformity was at issue, attempting to gain it by means of my-way-or-the-highway techniques, for example, held little appeal for the teacher/coach. "[The coach] must relate his teachings to basic problems and their solutions, rather than to aggressive 'do this or else' techniques." Nothing was learned by the tough-guy approach. "A forced response," he wrote, "by threats or violence is worthless at best." Daugherty wanted to reach his players, to leave a lasting impact. "The coach must understand and use psychological principles of adjustment and guidance techniques if he is to expect any semblance of adequate learning in his team personnel," he stated. "Without insight and concern, the athletic experience serves only as another stereotyped behavioral situation with little, if any, lasting value."

Again, hair length and style along with other superficial items were not measures of discipline for Daugherty. On the contrary, for the coach, discipline was much larger than external behavioral conformity to a specific set of rules. It had everything to do with a player's willingness to get in optimal physical condition, voluntarily pushing himself beyond his ordinary limits of endurance. The coach put a premium on penetrating conventional barriers of endurance to reach new levels of functioning. For him, it was an emotional commitment every bit as much as physical stamina that enabled an athlete to perform at peak effectiveness when he was already spent.

That Daugherty liked the saying "Adversity introduces a person to himself" is telling. Amid all the jocularity and fun, the man from coal-mining country knew life was serious and that success exacted a price. He had paid it long ago on his knees in the mines, when injured at Syracuse, and when facing potentially life-threatening circumstances in the military. Duffy had long ago been introduced to himself. Daugherty had to know that his black players had also been similarly introduced, particularly those that had endured the Jim Crow crucible of southern racism prior to enrolling at State. The coach also knew that, having surmounted the austerity of his own background, there was now steel inside his character, the type of steel that enables one to survive in the grimmest of circumstances. Now he wanted his players to develop similar strength, both physically and mentally. From a physical standpoint, this man who had spent months on his knees in the coal mines was focused on his players developing the strength necessary to stand strong in the fourth quarter, to dominate such that it would make his program—not even the most prestigious in his own state—vie for the top, not only in his conference, but in the nation.

Mentally, discipline meant a commitment to work hard, to sacrifice oneself in the cause of something greater than one's own self. He must have seen this very trait in his African American athletes when they were willing to put everything on the line to realize a step forward in social justice as it related to hiring practices at MSU. "A willingness to make a sacrifice for something bigger than the individual is the most unselfish trait a man can have," he noted in his autobiography. "I've never known a truly happy person who hasn't learned this lesson and made it a part of his life. I think if a man learns that his church, his family, his community, and his nation are more important than his own personal whims and wishes, he's on the right road to contentment in life." This was the lesson of football Duffy Daugherty hoped his players would learn. This was what real discipline consisted of to the coach. And the loquacious coach made certain every one of his teams knew that this was his credo. That latter knowledge was key to Daugherty's thinking. "If a coach is to expect any carry-over of his training to other than athletic competition, he must teach for it," he noted. In addition, "For the learning to be significant, the learner must understand the *why*, not just the *how*."

This was an era before year-round workouts. Accordingly, Daugherty wrote every player four letters. The first, sent in June, outlined a conditioning program to which he wanted him to adhere. The second letter, sent a month later, reviewed the team goals for the upcoming season, and these never changed: the Big Ten championship, a trip to the Rose Bowl, and the top spot in the nation. A third letter in August invited the players back to practice, and the final one beseeched the players to submit to the discipline associated with hard work, sacrifice for the larger cause, and commitment to exert themselves to the maximum in each practice as well as the games. These letters are telling. They reveal the essence of Daugherty's values. They make apparent that beneath that whimsical, don't-take-things-so-seriously surface was a bedrock set of beliefs about what was important in life and how football could be the classroom in which these cardinal truths could be learned.

That he wrote each player is also telling. This was not an era of email or easy mass communication. It was a time of carbon rather than photocopies. Each letter was indeed a personal communiqué and represented a brick in the bridge of what was perhaps Daugherty's greatest strength, his relationship with his athletes. He believed strongly that coaches had to allow for individual differences. "Though most teams must be spurred or driven," he wrote in *Defense Spartan Style*, "a coach must always be ready to recognize individual differences in response." He may have been referring to Smith when he noted, "He must spot individual problems and try to solve them in a matter that will best help the team." This attention to personal relationships was particularly important in the late 1960s, a time in which anyone over twenty-five was looked upon with suspicion. Interestingly, when Daugherty did decide to step down from coaching, he was again ahead of his time. It was not because the players had become too difficult to coach, or the student culture had become unmanageable. It was because he could no longer look these young men in the face—the ones from whom he was calling forth this sense of discipline—and tell them that they had a fighting chance to be the best. It was the system, not the players, with which he had differences. In that sense, he shared the same democratic spirit his players possessed, a desire for equal opportunity.

With the victory over Michigan, MSU carried a 3-2 record into its game at Iowa City. Moreover, with the Buckeyes and Wolverines in the rearview mirror and a 1-1 mark, the Spartans were in position to make a run at the conference title. The game against the Hawkeyes did nothing to encourage such hopes. Leading 18-12 with less than two minutes left, the State defense yielded a 6-yard TD pass from Mike Cilek to Kerry Reardon to tie the game at 18. Alan Schuette, who had already kicked second- and fourth-quarter field goals, then nailed the PAT and the Spartans went home stunned. An underachieving Indiana squad came to East Lansing the following week, led by quarterback Harry Gonso. It was the Hoosier defense, however, that surprised the Spartans, shutting them out 16-0. The loss was particularly bitter given that State came in averaging better than 23 points per game (never scoring less than 18).

While Daugherty enjoyed a comfortable relationship with his African American players amid a society riddled with racial anxiety, Indiana's Johnny Pont was feeling the pressure. On the following Wednesday, Pont dismissed ten black players for missing practice on successive days (an action Daugherty came very close to taking until President Hannah intervened in a similar situation at MSU). On Friday, the African Americans presented a list of grievances running from "inadequate medical treatment" to having "an atmosphere that is mentally depressing and normally discouraging for blacks." None of the charges were directed at Pont, who like Daugherty, had a favorable reputation regarding sensitive racial concerns. Although the unrest begs the question of what might have happened in East Lansing had Daugherty dropped boycotting black players from his squad, some believed that a Pont action may have precipitated the matter at Indiana. A month earlier the coach had shaken up his team, declaring all starting spots open, with the result being that a number of blacks lost their starting jobs and two African Americans were dropped from the traveling squad.

Four African American players had returned to practice on Wednesday, having missed only one day, and one—split end John Andrews—received a rousing ovation from Indiana fans in the Saturday game, though some members of the crowd were wearing "Go Big White" rather than "Go Big Red" buttons. The whole matter was intensified because the game was on regional television, with the dismissed blacks meeting in the Union Building during the game. Testimony to the volatile times, the university had eighty-four uniformed policemen surrounding the field, with a state police helicopter humming overhead.

Whether or not Daugherty had unwittingly trod perilously close to a confrontation with black athletes at Michigan State, the late 1960s were a time of such activism and protest, an era rife with incidents characterized by catharsis and the outpouring of anger over oppressive conditions, that no authority figure was immune to a public challenge of his or her authority. Coaches were at special risk for several reasons. In many football programs, blacks, though few in number, represented a much larger percentage of the team population than did African American students in general within the larger student body. Moreover, these African Americans were not fortunate to be in college; they had been recruited by the schools because of what they could do for the institution on the playing field. Finally, many of the coaches were "old school," authoritarian types, oceanically out of touch with the activist student of the time, particularly one of a different race.

A year after the Indiana flap, Syracuse icon Ben Schwartzwalder encountered an all-out revolt. It began publicly in the spring when the sixty-one-year-old broke an alleged promise to hire a black assistant. Nine African Americans walked out. Although the coach hired an African American at the direction of the university president, he told seven of the nine walkouts that they were dismissed from the squad. An eighth player then joined the protest. The players then filed a complaint with the Human Rights Commission, after which Schwartzwalder was ordered by the president to propose terms by which the players could be reinstated. When the terms were presented to the players, they rejected them, and with that the president supported their permanent dismissal.

Actually, the issue had been brewing for some time. Several years earlier a black student had been beaten by a white football player. Witnesses claimed the athlete had been attacked with a club, and the player simply exacted some street justice on the black student. In any case, charges were filed with the Human Rights Commission, and an uneasy peace hovered over the Syracuse program. When two vacancies emerged on the coaching staff, blacks asked that one be filled by an African American. Neither was, but Orangeman great Floyd Little helped out in spring practice. Little, an African American, sided with his former coach, criticizing the black players for their bitterness, and left after three days.

Four days later the black players began their boycott, the administration jumped in, and the once-proud Orangemen program became a cultural and political circus, with football as a sideshow. A clue to the problem can be found in Schwartzwalder's makeup. He had been a major in World War II. The tough, gravelly voiced mentor had received the Silver Star, Bronze Star, four battle stars, a Purple Heart, and a Presidential Unit Citation. In one sense, the aging mentor was a genuine hero. In another, he was an alien to college students now up in arms over an unpopular war in Southeast Asia. His attitude may have sealed his professional doom. "Some young kid I never saw before came into my office today. He asked me about that," said the coach, referring to an interaction with a reporter inquiring about the revolt of the black players. "I told him that I didn't talk to Communists, draft dodgers, flag burners, or people trying to destroy our country." When the reporter said he was none of these, the coach agreed to talk. His next comment, however, is starkly revealing. "I don't know what's happening anymore," he said. "I'm not supposed to be a football coach. I'm supposed to be a sociologist or something."

Ben Schwartzwalder's problem was less a matter of overt racism than simple cultural ignorance. He was a man of his time, a previous time, now in the eye of a sociopolitical storm characterized by rapid change. He longed to put time in a freeze-frame, to be a football coach in the classic sense of the term. Instead he was in charge of a group of athletes within a context he did not understand and had little tolerance for.

Daugherty's progressivism becomes much more visible when contrasted with that of Schwartzwalder. Duffy was a visionary, a man who liked new things, new experiences, whether in the form of a new offense or a new type of student-athlete. Life and change were not to be fought, they were to be accommodated if life was to be fun. Daugherty had rules, but far more important, this coach who emphasized the importance of individual differences had a desire to learn, to understand. He was ahead of the hands of time rather than invested in turning them back.

Daugherty had a particularly volatile mix during those years. He had a comparatively large number of African American players such that unhappy players could find solidarity in numbers. Moreover, the late 1960s was a time of rising expectations. Racial unrest was often most present in situations that, on the surface, appeared to be the least oppressive to minorities. Behavioral scientists theorized that the better (or perhaps the less oppressive) the conditions, the more particularly African Americans became conscious of the distance yet to be traveled. In any case, Daugherty was in the center of this, and that he survived as well as he did in the absence of consistent winning is a strong indicator of his comprehension of what was a confusing and often intimidating situation.

On the field, the Spartans were in a tailspin. After taking a 41-13 pounding from Purdue in West Lafayette, they returned home to play a below-average Minnesota squad. The Michigan State band played the theme of the popular television program *Mission: Impossible* and watched the Spartans disintegrate as two second-half fumbles led to a pair of Golden Gopher touchdowns, sending State to its fourth straight defeat, 14-10.

A 39-7 walloping of lowly Northwestern in Evanston closed the books on a 4-6 season. Duffy, now 12-18 over the past three years, needed a turnaround.

At 2-5, the Spartans did not stand out statistically in any Big Ten category other than, perhaps, in averaging more than a turnover a game more than the opposition. Their pass defense tied Purdue for worst in the league in yards per game (216.3), and the team was outscored by an average of nearly a touchdown a contest (5.6 points). Don Highsmith did rank 4th in rushing with 687 yards, while Pat Miller's 39.4 yards per punt was good for the #2 position. Eric "The Flea" Allen was 2nd in kickoff returns at 22.1 per attempt.

Guard Ron Saul was first-team all-league on offense, while twin Rich turned the same trick at defensive end, along with tackle Ron Curl. Linebacker Don Law made the second team.

CHAPTER 17

The Beginning of the End

**"Call an alumni meeting to hear a speech by someone from the geology
or English department, and the only way they can get a crowd is if the
guy shows X-rated movies. But get the football coach out to talk about his
upcoming team, and you'll turn 'em away."**

I n the 1970 season Duffy, only fifty-five, began thinking about getting out. Dr. Hannah, his principal backer, was gone. He had been replaced by Clifton R. Wharton Jr. There were no more frequent and supportive meetings, nor did the new president rely on Duffy's judgment on athletic matters; and for the first time the budget was an issue. In defense of Wharton, the times were tumultuous. The nation and its troubled campuses were coming off the unforgettable national spasms of 1968, and the country was knee-deep in the rice paddies of Vietnam, with hundreds of college-age youths dying weekly in a war growing in unpopularity. There was more on the president's plate than making it to Spartan Stadium on Saturday and basking in the glow of a State gridiron triumph.

Worse, however, is that the faculty representatives at each Big Ten school were gaining more and more power over the athletic programs, even though they were neither in the spotlight nor publicly accountable for program failure. The restrictions were growing such that it was becoming increasingly difficult to compete with schools from other conferences. "Maybe it's oversimplifying," Daugherty wrote in his autobiography, "but our Michigan State University teams weren't winning as often as I thought we should have, and winning had become more important than ever." Moreover, the budget and facilities at State were now lagging behind schools in its own conference. There appeared no light on the horizon for Daugherty, because the university seemed to be placing less and less importance on keeping the athletic program competitive, and "when victory becomes less important, victory becomes more infrequent." For Daugherty, a new unattractive trinity was emerging—administrative apathy, alumni discontent, and coaching frustration.

He was particularly nonplussed over the refusal to allow the practice of redshirting, permitting players to sit out their freshman year, while still giving them four years of eligibility. This four-seasons-over-five-years rule, one that enabled callow youths an extra year to mature, was widely practiced and to great advantage by the middle 1960s. Scholarship limits in the Big Ten, thirty per season, were more restrictive than in other major conferences. In fact, one procedure all but eliminated scholarships. It was called the need rule. An athlete's ability to pay was measured against the cost of a year at the institution. If, for example, the youngster's family could afford 10% of the costs, he would not get a full scholarship. He would get the other 90% of the cost.

Clearly, Big Ten teams were lagging behind the big dogs, having lost twenty-one straight games against Big Eight (now Big Twelve) teams. Although avoiding taking annual poundings from Big Eight powers, Duffy admittedly "didn't have the sense to avoid Southern California and Notre Dame and some others." In his retirement, Duffy described the situation as one in which solid Big Ten teams would have to play several of these nonconference behemoths, losing badly due to being outmanned. "By the time you got to your conference schedule," he wrote, "your record would be tarnished, along with your image. It would hurt your team emotionally and physically, rob your schedule of some of its luster." With the alumni, students, and media grumbling, it simply didn't mean much "if you went out and hammered Indiana after losing your first two games."

All this made recruiting more difficult. To tout the Big Ten's tradition of football excellence in appealing to a seventeen-year-old was "like trying to convince a man he should fight alongside you even though the whole world knows you're running low on ammunition." Duffy longed to have the control over his program that friends like John McKay at USC, Darrell Royal at Texas, and Bear Bryant at Alabama enjoyed.

And Duffy was tired of losing. He decided to shuffle the football deck at State, proceeding with a vengeance. "At Michigan State," wrote *Sports Illustrated*, "Duffy Daugherty has made more shifts than 'Bob and Carol and Ted and Alice.' The season opened inauspiciously at Washington, where the Spartans were clubbed 42-16 by an only slightly better than average Huskie team. A woeful Washington State squad was next, this one in East Lansing. State evened its record at 1-1 with a 28-14 triumph and looked toward its Spartan Stadium date with Notre Dame.

The Irish, who would finish the campaign 10-1, delivered a 29-0 shutout to the Spartans. It was Notre Dame's first win in East Lansing in twenty-nine years. A week later, Ohio State flattened the Green and White by an identical score. Asked to compare the two teams, Daugherty quipped, "They're obviously even. I suppose I'd have to vote one of them #1 and the other 1A." He may have been right, as Ohio State also finished 1970 with but a single loss. Bad as things were for Daugherty and his dispirited 1-3 Spartans, they looked to get worse. The next outing was on the road against another team that would win all but one in 1970, the Michigan Wolverines. Though not in a blowout, Bo's squad won convincingly, 34-20.

These were indeed crazy times. Students were brazen enough to revolt over seemingly any issue. Whereas black athletes had taken confrontational stands against coaches, at Illinois a curious reversal took place. When the Illinois Athletic Association fired coach Jim Valek in midseason (his record had been a dismal 7-29), Illini players voted unanimously to strike if Valek was not reinstated. "If Coach Valek is not here on Monday, Illinois does not have a football team," their resolution stated. The university buckled and Valek rode out his final campaign.

In any case, Duffy now faced a substantial challenge. Although the schedule figured to get easier—he would face a series of teams with losing records—unless the Spartans could summon some enthusiasm to finish out the campaign, he could be looking at his worst season ever, and this after going 12-18 in the previous three. The wily mentor called up a solid effort the following week against Iowa, defeating the Hawkeyes by a lopsided 37-0 score in East Lansing. Seven days later the Spartans were 3-4, dispatching the Hoosiers 32-7 at Indiana. By the first week of November, 1970 had become indeed a tale of two seasons as the Spartans evened their record at four up and four down with a 24-14 home conquest of Purdue.

Lowly Minnesota (3-6-1 for the year) was next. A victory in Paul Bunyan country would assure Daugherty no worse than a .500 campaign. A win there followed by a season-ending victory at home over Northwestern would give the Green and White a 6-4 year, having finished the season with five straight wins.

No team gave Duffy more headaches than Minnesota. He was 2-8 against the Gophers going into the 1970 season, by far his worst mark against a conference foe. After the game he was 2-9, as the struggling Minnesota team put the Spartans away, 23-13. It would now take a home win over Northwestern to even the season record.

"Let's talk about this game, not the Rose Bowl. This was the big game for us," said Wildcat coach Alex Agase after edging MSU, 23-20. Although Ohio State secured the bid to Pasadena, Agase was elated. "Look, it's beautiful, it's beautiful to be 6-1 in the Big Ten. This is only the second time in history Northwestern has won six conference games. And it's nice to be thought about."

It was not beautiful for Daugherty, and the Spartan fans were not having happy thoughts about him and his program. The loss capped four straight nonwinning seasons, a stretch during which he had gone 16-24, a calamitous comedown from the 29-8-2 mark of the four before that. It had been an ugly loss. All–Big Ten quarterback Maurie Daigneau had fired two TD strikes to flanker Barry Pearson off fakes on which the Spartan defenders had bitten. Mike Adamle, the Wildcats' prize back, had rumbled 137 yards though the State defense. Then, with the game knotted at 20, Bill Planisek hit on his third field goal to drown the Spartans near the Red Cedar River.

At 3-4, one would not have expected the Spartans to distinguish themselves in the league numbers, but the team did rank #3 in total defense and second in both offensive and defensive passing yards. Eric Allen was 3rd in rushing with 787 yards, and also 3rd in kickoff returns (18.6 yards per return). Mike Rasmussen was 4th in passing rating. On defense, middle guard Ernie Hamilton and linebacker Mike Hogan combined for fifteen tackles for loss. On offense, end Gordon Bowdell, guard Joe DeLamielleure, and center Tom Beard joined Allen on the second-team All–Big Ten squad. There were no Spartans on either defensive unit.

CHAPTER 18

Frustration

**"My fears really got out of hand when there was a fumble near our bench
and the referee dived down into the middle of the pile and screamed, 'I've
got it . . . it's our ball.'"**

—Duffy on encountering an official with an Irish surname in a game with Notre Dame

Just five years after being at the top of his profession, Duffy Daugherty was now
in trouble. Rumors were swirling that the once-celebrated symbol of football
and PR brilliance was one losing season from coaching extinction. Of course,
the genial Irishman was optimistic. Despite decaying facilities, a shrinking football
budget, and the absence of a president in his corner, he had some players like Brad
Van Pelt and Eric "The Flea" Allen around which to build.

While many were writing him off as a fossil, a now prematurely old dreamer,
upon closer examination one could argue that Daugherty's irrepressible optimism
contributed greatly to his professional success. Many Big Ten coaches had come and
gone since his taking over in 1954, often in programs that had much more going for
them than the one in East Lansing. Daugherty had managed to take the state's second

university not only to the top of Michigan, but to the top of the conference and nation. It took vision and optimism to do that. Clearly, had the coach adopted a more "realistic" outlook back in 1954, he would have been long gone by 1971. How else but through the energy born of a can-do optimism could the former coal miner have recruited with the vigor he displayed? How else could a man from a provincial rural background summon the daring to blaze recruiting trails among African American youngsters from the South, convincing them and their skeptical parents that life in East Lansing, Michigan, would be good for them?

So Duffy put aside the negatives and went at it in 1971 amid the doubters and those already feeling he had overstayed his welcome. The Spartans opened their now eleven-game campaign at home against Illinois, in a rebuilding year under new coach Bob Blackman, and came away with a solid 10-0 win. Game two would send the Spartans south to play Georgia Tech in another winnable game. The denizens of the press box talked of dedicating the grind-it-out contest to Tech hero Lewis Clark, who had played before the forward pass was legalized. Incredibly, the home team did not complete a single pass (the Yellow Jackets were 0 for 10 with one interception), yet prevailed by the same 10-0 score by which State had won against Illinois. It was an extraordinarily frustrating game for MSU, as the Spartans endured four interceptions, and twice were stopped on fourth down and short yardage. "Oh, just for a couple of feet or more here or there," the coach who was that close to being 2-0 moaned.

A mediocre Oregon State cooperated with the Spartans' gridiron wishes the following week, as the Green and White cruised to a 31-14 win. The food was pretty tasty for the coach that evening as the triumph marked Daugherty's one hundredth win against only sixty losses and four ties.

With now some basis for optimism, MSU headed for South Bend and the annual confrontation with Notre Dame. Gone were the up-and-down years of the past, as Parseghian had built a real juggernaut at the Catholic school, a program that hadn't seen a losing season since the Armenian mentor had arrived from Northwestern in 1964. This team, destined to go 8-2, was no exception. The game went to the Irish by a 14-2 count, and Duffy was incensed with the zebras who he felt had been treating his invading Spartans to some home cooking. The officials had flagged State's receivers for blocking defenders before the intended receiver had caught the ball, roughly tantamount to a moving pick in hoops. Viewing it as equivalent to a parking violation, Daugherty said sarcastically, "I've seen it called once every 10 years."

It didn't end there for the angry coach. This sin of commission was matched by one of omission, in Daugherty's opinion. The refs had ignored two seemingly apparent roughing-the-kicker misdeeds on the part of the Irish, something the irate mentor pointed out while standing several yards on the playing field. It didn't matter. The game went into the books as a Spartan loss, and Duffy was back at .500.

Michigan, now an annual national power under Schembechler, came to East Lansing a week later. They left with a 24-13 win, as Bill Taylor rushed for 117 yards on just fifteen attempts despite injuring his shoulder in the first half. After Notre Dame and Michigan, State was happy Wisconsin, a school with seven consecutive losing seasons, was next in Madison. Eric "The Flea" Allen ran wild in Camp Randall, rolling up 247 yards and two touchdowns. It was not enough, as the Badgers' Roger Jaeger's late field goal gave the home team a 31-28 win. "We've finally won the one we weren't supposed to," said a jubilant John Jardine, Badger coach. For Duffy it was the opposite. He had lost one he was not supposed to. The season was becoming increasingly frustrating. Had the Spartans taken care of gridiron business in this one and at Georgia Tech, the team would have been 4-2. With better cooperation from the men in stripes at South Bend, the Green and White might have been 5-1 and the talk of the nation. But they weren't 5-1 or 4-2. They weren't even 3-3. They were 2-4, just a pair of losses away from yet another losing season.

Fortunately a hapless (1-10 for the season) Iowa team came in next and rolled over as the Spartans took out their frustrations on the visitors to the tune of 34-3. Eric Allen then exploded at Purdue for 350 rushing yards (an NCAA record) on twenty-nine carries, and State glided to a resounding 43-10 victory in a most opportunistic fashion. The Spartans turned four fumbles and one Purdue interception into four TDs and a field goal.

The victory road figured to come to a halt the following week in the Horseshoe in Columbus, Ohio. But it didn't. Down 10-3 in the third quarter, Spartan ace Brad Van Pelt picked off a Buckeye aerial and returned it to the Ohio State seven. Two plays later Allen went over from the five. In the fourth quarter, disaster struck again for Woody Hayes's charges as State's Doug Halliday fell on an errant pitchout at the Buckeye eleven. Four plays later Allen was in the end zone for the winning score. "We gave them the ball in too good a field position," said Hayes, stating the obvious.

Pesky Minnesota was next for the 5-4 Spartans. In a 65-point shootout, "The Flea" scored four times to lift the Green and White to a 40-25 win at Spartan Stadium. Duffy had done it again. His unquenchable optimism, his refusal to roll over and write off the season, and his willingness to make adjustments had brought this 1971 contingent from the brink of football disaster to a 6-4 record.

The final game was played in Evanston against a similar 6-4 Northwestern team, riding the good feeling of putting together back-to-back winning campaigns after years of gridiron ineptitude. The Wildcats seized the momentum by getting into the end zone on their initial possession, while keeping the ball for nearly ten minutes in the first quarter. The Northwestern defense held Allen and his mates to just 7 points, after they had averaged more than 32 points per outing in their previous five contests, as the Wildcats registered a decisive 28-7 victory.

It had been a season of frustration. The 5-3 Spartans, who outscored their league rivals by an average of 7.4 points per game, were strong on offense, ranking 1st overall and 2nd in rushing. They were 4th in both rushing and overall defense; 2nd in passing yards. Eric Allen ran away with the rushing crown, totaling 1,283 yards at 6.1 a carry, and scored a league-leading 110 points. Mike Rasmussen was rated 8th in passing.

Guard Joe DeLamielleure joined Allen on the first-team All–Big Ten offensive unit, with end Billy DuPree on the second. Defensive back Brad Van Pelt made the first and linebacker Ernie Hamilton the second defensive team.

CHAPTER 19

The Final Season

"I hope you can get a new coach as good as me."

—Duffy's words to Athletic Director Burt Smith near the end of Daugherty's final season

By 1972, with the ever-growing burdens of coaching in what was now a less hospitable, more restrictive environment at State, Daugherty was giving serious consideration to putting down his coaching whistle and beginning another football-related career. Although Eric Allen and his better than 1,500 yards rushing were gone, State had some good underclassmen to augment tight end Billy Joe DuPree and roving safety Brad Van Pelt, so Daugherty felt his usual flush of optimism as the team practiced in earnest that fall.

The Spartans responded to their fifty-seven-year-old mentor with a 24-0 shutout of the Illini in Champaign-Urbana. The spirited Spartans sealed the Illini on their half of the field the entire game. With Illini quarterback Mike Wells out with an injured finger, Illinois was forced to the overland route, but without success. The defense scored two TDs and set up the third. Believing that teams improve the most between their first and second games of the season, Daugherty was confident that his squad would leave its mark in 1972.

They didn't. An inferior Georgia Tech team came to East Lansing and upended the Spartans 21-16. Eddie McAshan, the Georgia Tech quarterback, threw over what amounted to a nine-man MSU defensive line at Spartan Stadium. McAshan hit on a TD strike of 77 yards to Jim Robinson on the first play from scrimmage. He added another thirty-six-yarder to the same receiver among his sixteen completions in twenty-six attempts. "They shocked us on the first play," said Duffy, "and we stayed in a state of shock all day."

Why did it happen? Who was to blame? Daugherty's response in his book provides an insight into the dyspeptic nature of his mind-set. "A piece of it goes to everybody. Obviously our staff didn't have our team ready, and I'm not sure I can understand why. Perhaps all of us had been demoralized by that time because of the limitations placed on us within the conference and the university and the sniping from the old grads."

The team then headed to Los Angeles, where the Spartans took a 51-6 pounding from USC, the best in the West and en route to an undefeated season. State helped the Trojan cause by fumbling five times and throwing three interceptions. "You must remember," said USC mentor John McKay rather graciously, "when one team is hitting another team like we were hitting Michigan State—from all angles and all sides—they are going to cough up the football." He had praise for State. "We beat a good team, and we played a great defensive game, maybe the best defense in a long time."

There was hope, however, as the Irish were coming to East Lansing the following Saturday. A win over Ara's bunch, a school against which Duffy had gone 10-6-1 over the years, could turn the season around. The folks in East Lansing still believed, as 77,828 fans made their way into Spartan Stadium for a game against mighty Notre Dame. Despite the 51-6 annihilation of the previous week, and having to use a converted cornerback, Mark Niesen at quarterback, Duffy's team dug in against nearly insurmountable odds. It took three Bob Thomas field goals and a last-second 8-yard TD by Andy Huff to subdue State 16-0. There was simply no offense for State in this nationally televised encounter. Never penetrating beyond the Irish 44, the Spartans punted more times (ten) than they passed (nine) in a mistake-ridden day.

Now a dismal 1-3, Duffy headed into the lion's den of the Big Ten—Michigan Stadium—to face a Wolverine squad that would go 10-1 for the season. Again, a superb defensive effort was wasted in a crushing 10-0 loss before 103,735 partisans. Nothing broke the Spartans' way. A 24-yard TD run by Niesen was wiped out on a clipping penalty, and then running back David Brown was hit by Wolverine namesake safety Dave Brown on the Michigan three and had the ball pop out and into the end zone for a touchback. With nine minutes left in the contest, State had the ball, 4th and 1, on the Michigan 40. The score was just 3-0. Duffy gambled, running an end sweep. It was stopped and followed by a Michigan end-around that went 58 yards for the clinching touchdown.

The loss to Schembechler's squad was a particularly bitter one. Although failing to complete a single pass—at least to any Spartan, as three were picked off by Michigan—State should have won. The team rendered a valiant effort, good enough to win, but took the defeat in part owing to several officiating blunders. One took away a Spartan TD in the second quarter, and another gave the Wolverines an undeserved score in the final quarter. The calls were bad enough for the commissioner's office to call Daugherty to acknowledge the officiating ineptitude. Confession, though good for the soul, does not rise to the level of turning a defeat into a victory, and as Duffy put it, "I never could get Bo to reverse that score and put it down as a victory for Michigan State," so State was now 1-4.

Daugherty and his staff were now looking in the face of a truly disastrous campaign, this after five seasons of never winning more than six games. The 1965–66 era seemed a century ago. More specifically, Duffy's teams had gone a remarkable 82-35-4 over his first thirteen seasons at the Spartan helm. He was just 22-29 since. With all hope for respectability apparently gone, Daugherty, having lost four straight to national powers, rallied his squad a week later for a game against a middling Badger squad. The specter of a home loss to Wisconsin was unthinkable, particularly with the likes of Purdue and Ohio State still ahead. Somehow, the Spartans recovered their energies and routed the Badgers, 31-0.

The sky was brightening. A win over a weak Iowa squad the following week would pull State to within a game of .500 overall and make the Spartans a solid 3-1 in Big Ten play. So goes the roller-coaster nature of big-time college football.

Once again, the offense took the week off, and mistakes cost the Spartans a win in Iowa City. The Spartans left town with nothing but a 6-6 tie against a Hawkeye team that would win only three games all season. State lost an unthinkable five fumbles in a game in which Hawkeye kicker Harry Kokolus delivered his second field goal of the game in the fourth quarter to deny State the win.

It was now a season of might-have-beens. The usually irrepressible Daugherty saw the Michigan travesty as the turnaround point in the team's fortunes. "I'll always believe that had we gotten the victory we deserved over Michigan," he later wrote, "we never would have been tied by Iowa—and even with all the disappointments of my final season, we still could have won the conference championship."

For Duffy, there were no more straws. He told his bride, Francie, that this was his final season on the sidelines. Her reaction was typical of her lovely character. Whatever Duffy wanted was fine with her. Daugherty informed his staff on Sunday night. He spoke to his team the following day. "This game is supposed to be fun," he recalled telling the team, "and I haven't succeeded in making it fun for you this year." After making several other points, he returned to his principal text. "Fun in football comes from doing things together as a team, having success as a team, and knowing you have played well and given the utmost of yourselves. This feeling transcends all else and is much more vital than individual accomplishment. Because I haven't been able to make football fun for you fellows, I am resigning at the end of the 1972 season."

Then Duffy became Duffy again. "But from now until the end of the season, it's going to be fun. Now, we play Purdue on Saturday. Purdue is a big, tough team, and if we're going to win on Saturday, we're going to have to walk with a growl all week." True to form, Daugherty promised to tell the team a joke before every practice. His initial story illustrated the importance of being tough rather than merely looking tough. He told the squad of a fictional cowboy who tied his horse on the rail as he headed into the saloon for a few belts. When he went back outside, he noticed that someone had painted his horse's testicles a rich purple. Enraged, he hitched up his gunbelt, made certain his six-shooters were ready, and strode confidently back into the bar. He went to the center of the room and with his hands on his six-shooters bellowed, "OK, where's the clown who did the paint job on my horse? Stand up and take your punishment like a man."

One fellow arose from his chair—in stages. He was a 6'8" 280-pound Goliath. "I painted your horse. What are you going to do about it?"

The cowboy dropped his hands from his guns and said in little more than a weak whisper, "I just thought I'd tell you the first coat is just about dry."

One who remembered that time well was future Notre Dame coach Ty Willingham. Willingham, all of 5' 6" as a high school player, had seen fellow Fayetteville, North Carolina, native Jimmy Raye barking signals as a black signal caller in 1966. Willingham longed to play for the man who was ahead of his time, one who was colorblind when it came to race and position. Willingham recruited Daugherty. "I sent Duffy 100 letters, all hand-written, asking to be a walk-on," said Willingham. Jimmy Raye was one of Duffy's assistants at the time. "That was my connection," he stated.

He walked on, and though Willingham was a redshirt in 1972, Duffy's profile looms large in Willingham's memory. "I still remember my first practice with Duffy, when he called the team together and told us a joke," Willingham mused. "What a legend!"

"We wanted him to go out a winner," said Brad Van Pelt. "You could see it in the guys' faces." The Spartans, realizing that this was Duffy's last go-round, doused visiting Purdue's Rose Bowl hopes 22-12. Mark Niesen scored on runs of 57 and 61 yards. On defense, the hurrying Spartans buried Boilermaker quarterback Gary Danielson for 60 yards in losses.

Despite the stirring win, two missed field goals and blown PAT were of concern to Duffy, so he decided to change kickers for the upcoming game against nearly omnipotent Ohio State. He turned to a foreign-born (the Netherlands) walk-on, Dirk Krijt. The youngster, with a shoulder-length mane, had approached Duffy after the season was well under way. He was a soccer-style kicker with a boom in his legs, and Daugherty elevated him to the varsity so late that his name did not appear in the game program.

Indeed, Duffy's "little Dutch treat" was the key to the momentous 19-12 upset of the Ohio State Buckeyes. The 165-pound kicker hit on four field goals in his debut. "They had a tryout, and they hired me right away," said Krijt with delicious political incorrectness. With the game 12-12 at the half on all four Krijt conversions, Mark Niesen took advantage of one of Ohio State's five turnovers and scored on a six-yard run. The Buckeyes managed only 107 yards rushing. "We took a real good whipping from them, and we deserved it," said a glum Woody Hayes.

With the press crowded around Duffy in the locker room, Krijt ambled by, openly smoking a cigarette. It didn't end there. The new Spartan hero then informed his coach audibly, "Coach, I'm going to go out tonight and celebrate with a girl and have a couple of beers. You want to come along?"

Hoping none of the assembled press would identify Krijt as the team's kicking hero, Daugherty attempted to ignore the incident. It didn't work, as one of the scribes asked if indeed that had been Krijt. Once his identity was confirmed, questions pertaining to training rules followed quickly.

At his best in extemporaneous situations, Duffy asserted, "We have a new rule. Anyone who can kick four field goals in one game is allowed to do most anything he likes."

Krijt graduated from MSU and returned to Europe. There he made some critical remarks about the overemphasis on football in the United States, objecting to its violent, competitive nature. The former coal miner turned football coach took exception in his book, saying, "There is something truly beautiful about getting down on your hands and knees and digging and scraping for something you really want, even if it's something like one simple victory."

In any case, in a season filled with unpredictability, the Spartans did the nearly impossible. They had managed to hang on against an Ohio State team that would only lose one other game all season.

Duffy had never won in Minneapolis before 1972, and he didn't win after either. In his final game in the Gopher Hole, a 36-yard return of an intercepted lateral was key in a 14-10 defeat. Perhaps the team did not recover from the high of the Buckeye triumph quickly enough, but the players' promise to send their coach out on a winning season fell short, just short—the Spartans were stopped twice on fourth-down plays at the Minnesota three in the game's final period.

The coaching career of Duffy Daugherty ended with a solid 24-14 win over Northwestern. State scored three times in the opening period, two coming on passes less than a minute apart. Niesen, who came in having completed ten of fifty-one as a passer, went five for eight for 167 yards and added a third TD on a 7-yard run. It was Daugherty's 109th win and the school's 400th. "I really haven't had time to reflect on this," he said. "I suppose the nostalgic feeling hasn't had time to sink in, but I'm not sad. I only have a feeling of gratitude toward the team."

Duffy had closed in a blaze of glory. After starting 1-4, his Spartans closed 4-1-1 to get Daugherty to a .500 (5-5-1) campaign overall, and a very solid 5-2-1 in the Big Ten. The team went 3-1 after the coach's retirement announcement.

State ranked 2nd in league rushing on both sides of the ball. Scoring exactly twice as many points as their foes (136-68), the Green and White ranked 4th in total defense. David Brown was 5th in rushing at 565 yards, and Bill Simpson led the loop in punt returning (11.2 per attempt). Paul Hayner and Simpson were 1-2 in interceptions, combining for nine, while Simpson was the second-best punter in the Big Ten with a 39.7 average. John Shinsky was the league's best in tackles for loss with a dozen; Hamilton and Chris King tied for third. Simpson tied for first in breaking up passes (6), while teammate Hayner was knotted for 4th.

Billy Joe DuPree and Joe DeLamielleure made the first team all-conference on offense. Tackle James Nicholson was on the second squad. Defensive backs Simpson and All-American Brad Van Pelt in addition to linebacker Gail Clark were first-team on defense. End Brian McConnell and tackle Gary Van Elst made the second team.

For Duffy Daugherty, it was a sweet way to go out. "It's been said there are only two kinds of coaches—those who have been fired, and those who are going to be fired," he later remarked. "I was one of the lucky ones."

CHAPTER 20

Life after Coaching

"There are two things that can happen if you stay [coaching] in one spot too long. You'll get fired, or you'll get hemorrhoids, or both."

When Daugherty did decide to step down, he was again ahead of his time. It was not because the players had become too difficult to coach, or the student culture had become unmanageable, or that he was deemed no longer able to coach effectively. It was because he could no longer look these young men in the face—the ones from whom he was calling forth discipline and commitment—and tell them that they had a fighting chance to be the best. It was the system, not the players, with which he had differences. In that sense, he shared the same democratic spirit his players possessed, a desire for equal opportunity.

One of the first things Daugherty did was go to work on his autobiography, a book published just two years after his retirement. That he wrote it (with Dave Diles) so soon was probably a mistake. The rather short book is uproariously funny and contains some very solid football observations, as well as some insights into Daugherty's personality. The book does, however, have a bitter tone running through much of it, a "sour grapes" quality that may not have been present had Daugherty had the benefit of greater hindsight in describing the conditions he found objectionable. It is safe to assume that what comes off as bitterness more likely masks a deep hurt—a wound that was a bit too fresh for Daugherty to begin chronicling his Michigan State experience within months of his coaching departure.

Daugherty notes that despite the fine finish to the season, he spoke with Athletic Director Burt Smith and with university executive vice president Jack Breslin about the state of the football program in which he had been working. He pointed out that the quality of State's facilities exceeded only those of lowly Northwestern. The school did not even have a meeting room to show movies to the squad. Moreover, Michigan State coaching salaries ranked ninth in the league, as did the overall football budget. He railed away at the Big Ten and Michigan State under Wharton in his autobiography, lamenting that the Big Ten, once "the pride of the nation in football," through indifference had permitted its football representatives to degenerate into "second-rate performers." He referred to the administrators and faculty representatives as "mid-Victorian thinkers. Some aren't thinkers at all."

For Daugherty it was sad that giants such as Fritz Crisler, Biggie Munn, Red Mackey, Ivy Williamson, and Stu Holcomb (and though left unwritten, most certainly, Duffy Daugherty) had had the control of the gridiron programs taken from them. "That's because the Big Ten really isn't the Big Ten," he recorded. "It's called the 'Western Intercollegiate Athletic Association of Faculty Representatives'—that's the official title, and the faculty folks have taken great delight in letting people know they were in charge." For Duffy, giving such people authority over a university's football program was tantamount to "putting caddies in charge of golf greens." For Daugherty, these people lacked two things—vision and courage. Although he didn't mention it, these were two things even the most casual observer would note had characterized his life.

Daugherty had long opposed the no-repeat rule in the Rose Bowl, a long-standing restriction. "For what seemed like centuries," the faculty reps stood strong on the no-repeat rule, arguing that it would be academically disruptive for a group of players to go to the Rose Bowl in successive seasons. Daugherty noted, however, that the faculty reps showed up in Pasadena annually, with their expenses paid. "Apparently it would have disrupted studying, but not teaching," he noted in sarcasm. As for university president Wharton, he faced none of the pressure to win that the football coach encountered. "Did you ever hear of a president getting fired for an inadequate athletic program?" Duffy groused.

The whole matter had become unmanageable for the usually genial gridiron mentor. Almost no one understood. "And it's safe to say," he wrote, "that only a small fraction of the old grads understand that the coach had an administrator who wanted to win within the rules, a conference that made it impossible to compete on equal footing, a faculty rep who figured winning too much was a sin, an athletic director who was helpless, and a press that never could understand why you didn't go 10-0 every season."

It had to hurt. Daugherty came in under a cloud, as Biggie Munn's boy. By 1958, five years after he had been established as head coach, Daugherty once again felt the sting of dismissal when an understandably angry Munn charged him with allowing the program to tumble down and go "to pieces." The determined Daugherty followed that disappointment by elevating the program to incredible heights in 1965 and 1966, only to watch his competitive opportunities gradually erode until he directed an at best mediocre program, no longer with the unqualified support of the university president, and without the attention of an adoring press and the adulation of the Spartan fans. Moreover, after a nineteen-year tenure of remaining faithful to the Green and White in the face of extraordinarily attractive opportunities to coach elsewhere, it ended with his leaving on an unsatisfying note, one marked by mediocrity and with many State adherents happy to see him go.

Daugherty knew he had stayed too long. Had he left State five or six years earlier, with the program on top, he might have parlayed that success into a second career at a university that was more conducive to keeping its football program competitive. But Duffy Daugherty had two characteristics, if no others: he was optimistic and he was loyal. He never saw the glass half empty—with a break here or a break there, he saw every team he coached as Big Ten champions. Additionally, his circle of friends remained the same through the decades, his loyalty to his family only deepened, and he had turned down a number of plum coaching opportunities over the years.

Nonetheless, he had had a bellyful. He "grew to hate recruiting" and tired of fending off criticism from a less than adoring press and alumni. No one who enjoyed attention as much as Daugherty could do so without a substantial ego. Under the whimsical, life-is-fun exterior lay a highly competitive personality, one that had become accustomed to success. To be trudging along in the middle of the Big Ten pack during his last six campaigns was a painful comedown for a coach who had never experienced even two consecutive nonwinning seasons in his first twenty years as a member of the Michigan State coaching staff. It was a long way down, from being featured on the cover of *Time* and in *Sports Illustrated* to being all but ignored on the national front.

One cannot help but get the impression—in reviewing Daugherty's comments—that although he would never have admitted it, he never felt he got his due. Too often Daugherty was presented as a comedian, a gridiron carnival barker, who did a little coaching on the side, rather than a man who succeeded in keeping the state's less-celebrated university more than competitive for nineteen years, a coach who finished with a combined 20-14-3 mark against Michigan and Notre Dame, and who posted a .500 or better record in the Big Ten for eleven of his first thirteen years. Four of his six conference-losing seasons occurred after 1966, during his final seasons, a time when his program suffered from deteriorating facilities and eventually the league's second-lowest football budget. Even so, Daugherty never went less than 2-5, and twice 3-4; in his final two Big Ten campaigns the coach posted a 10-5-1 mark.

It wasn't age—Daugherty was just fifty-seven when he stepped down. Nonetheless, by 1972 he showed all the signs of burnout. Football coaching was no longer fun, the enthusiasm gone. He seemed older than his years, perhaps because of his prematurely white hair and the sheer length of his MSU tenure. One wonders what might have happened had Daugherty taken over elsewhere after a year or two respite. That, however, was a time when sixty was old, very old. The era of the ageless coach, of Bill Parcells, Dick Vermeil, Joe Gibbs, Bobby Bowden, and Joe Paterno had not yet arrived. Duffy's days in the sun were over.

Nonetheless, Duffy's favorite colors were green and white, and so he remained after the 1972 season and became Assistant to the Vice President in Charge of Development. The supreme self-promoter and promoter of his football program was now promoting Michigan State University. He was a fund-raiser.

Deploring a make-work position, Daugherty felt good about the job. Michigan State was in his veins and he was happy to sell it to wealthy contributors. He also joined the ABC football crew. Ever the ham, it put Daugherty and his endless passel of stories in national view. Besides, he was always available for personal appearances, public speaking, or as a participant in football clinics.

In time his legend has grown. In the twenty-seven years from Duffy's retirement to the end of the millennium, Michigan State employed no less than five coaches. Their combined record was a barely over .500 mark of 156-145-8. The longest tenure belonged to George Perles, twelve years, during which he went 68-67-4. No other coach lasted more than five seasons.

But for Duffy it was about so much more than coaching. It was about an exciting life far away from the coal mines of Pennsylvania. It was about a family he loved intensely, and other people about which he cared deeply. It was also about doing the right thing and speaking up for just causes. His daughter Dree noted her father's pioneering recruiting ventures, something that came to full flower in the turbulent 1960s, and his support for African American athletes. "The most important thing my father did was to influence society on race relations," Duffy's daughter said proudly. "Michigan State was the first major college to have black football players in starting and star positions."

Hugh Daugherty, coach, entertainer, raconteur, and trailblazer. The boy from Barnesboro was so far ahead of his time that his style fits far better in the media-driven culture of today than that of the 1960s and 1970s. He valued diversity before the word had a political connotation. Gone since 1987, he was so far ahead of his time he was not adequately appreciated until after his time. Now, with athletic facilities and awards bearing his name, he looms larger than ever.

"Duffy"—we will not see his like again.

INDEX